teria cook, accountant or computer programmer, you have been anointed by God to do what you are doing. This anointment does not mean that you are stuck in place for the rest of your life, forced by God into a job that you may or may not enjoy. No, not at all. Knowing and accepting that you are anointed for the position you presently hold simply means trusting that you are on a journey and that there is something you need to learn and take with you from your present position into your next stop along the way. And I'm convinced that these lessons are both skill-building as well as character-building. You may need to learn computer skills such as using Excel and Microsoft Word as well as patience and gratitude. You may need to learn how to manage a team of people as well as how to manage your temper.

For those who know and love the Lord, I am convinced that nothing is wasted in this life. Even what we throw away ourselves, God often reaches down and redeems into something of merit, beauty, and usefulness. "And we know that all things work together for good to those who love God, to those who are the called according to *His* purpose" (Romans 8:28). Certainly, it is sometimes difficult to see this in the moment. When Eve discovered the horror that one of her sons had murdered the other, and that Cain would be punished by God accordingly, she could not see ahead and know her next son, Seth, would establish the line leading to the birth of Jesus. When Joseph was sold into slavery by his brothers, he could not see ahead to know that God would turn their evil inten-

well past retirement age so that their grandchildren could attend college? How many prayers did your mother lift up for you to stay in school? How many teachers stayed after school to make sure you understood the necessary concepts and principles that would ensure your advancement?

It's far too easy to complain and grumble about your present position, whether it be as night shift cashier at the 7-Eleven or CEO of a Fortune 500 company, without appreciating how you got there. I encourage you to spend some time, before you go any further, reflecting on and giving thanks for all of the contributions that your families, friends, teachers, coaches, and mentors have made in your life. Perhaps they have not given you exactly what you would like or as much as you'd like, but all of us have received something that enables us to be where we are at this present moment.

I exhort you to release any notion of victimhood that may be stalking your mind, laying claim to your peace and robbing you of your contentment. Your agony might have been your ancestors' ecstasy. Your job, in spite of all of its problems, would have been the dream of our forefathers. In fact, many of you may have prayed over the application to get the job that you now loathe. God is no respecter of persons; you are not entitled to a life of independent wealth and irresponsibility. Every gimme has a gotcha and when all is said and done, no one wins by accident.

As difficult as it may be to accept, you are in your present position for a reason. Yes, whether working as a janitor or cafe-

THE TEN COMMANDMENTS OF WORKING IN A HOSTILE ENVIRONMENT

T. D. Jakes

The Ten Commandments of Working in a Hostile Environment

BERKLEY BOOKS, NEW YORK

THE BERKLEY PUBLISHING GROUP
Published by the Penguin Group
Penguin Group (USA) Inc.
375 Hudson Street, New York, New York 10014, USA
Penguin Group (Canada), 10 Alcorn Avenue, Toronto, Ontario M4V 3B2, Canada
(a division of Pearson Penguin Canada Inc.)
Penguin Books Ltd., 80 Strand, London WC2R 0RL, England
Penguin Group Ireland, 25 St. Stephen's Green, Dublin 2, Ireland (a division of Penguin Books Ltd.)
Penguin Group (Australia), 250 Camberwell Road, Camberwell, Victoria 3124, Australia
(a division of Pearson Australia Group Pty. Ltd.)
Penguin Books India Pvt. Ltd., 11 Community Centre, Panchsheel Park, New Delhi—110 017, India
Penguin Group (NZ), cnr Airborne and Rosedale Roads, Albany, Auckland, New Zealand
(a division of Pearson New Zealand Ltd.)
Penguin Books (South Africa) (Pty.) Ltd., 24 Sturdee Avenue, Rosebank, Johannesburg 2196, South Africa

Penguin Books Ltd., Registered Offices: 80 Strand, London WC2R 0RL, England

This book is an original publication of The Berkley Publishing Group.

THE TEN COMMANDMENTS OF WORKING
IN A HOSTILE ENVIRONMENT

PRINTING HISTORY
Berkley hardcover edition / January 2005
Berkley hardcover ISBN: 0-425-20016-7

This book has been catalogued with the Library of Congress.

PRINTED IN THE UNITED STATES OF AMERICA

10   9   8   7   6   5   4   3   2   1

CONTENTS

Introduction: Help Wanted

1

FIRST COMMANDMENT:
KNOW THAT YOU ARE ANOINTED
FOR THE JOB OR POSITION YOU NOW HOLD!

9

SECOND COMMANDMENT:
DON'T EXPECT TO BE APPRECIATED

33

THIRD COMMANDMENT:
EMBRACE OPPORTUNITIES FOR CHANGE

49

FOURTH COMMANDMENT:
DO THE JOB WELL WHILE REMEMBERING
THE VISION

69

v

CONTENTS

FIFTH COMMANDMENT:
DON'T LET THE ENVIRONMENT GET INSIDE OF YOU!
87

SIXTH COMMANDMENT:
INCREASE YOUR CAPACITY TO WORK WITH DIFFICULT PERSONALITIES
111

SEVENTH COMMANDMENT:
WHERE YOU ARE IS NOT WHERE YOU ARE GOING!
133

EIGHTH COMMANDMENT:
ACHIEVE OPTIMAL RESULTS WITH MINIMAL CONFUSION
157

NINTH COMMANDMENT:
DO NOT PLEDGE ALLEGIANCE TO CLIQUES AND GROUPS!
177

TENTH COMMANDMENT:
ALWAYS KEEP YOUR SONG NEAR YOU
195

Conclusion: Exit Interview
211

HELP WANTED

ACCORDING to most sources, you will spend over half your waking life on the job. Think about that for just a moment—*over half your life*. That's more time than you spend at home with those you love the most! Imagine sitting at your desk amidst all the spreadsheets, hiding out in your cubicle with your keyboard, or sweating in the factory on the assembly line year after year after year. While most experts agree that the average adult will only spend about seven years with the same employer before changing jobs, this is still an astounding amount of time spent in any one workplace. And from what I've experienced myself, working as a

janitor, a factory worker, a hardware store manager, a salesman, a pastor, and an entrepreneur, I know what it's like to experience trials on the job. If you don't like your job and the
hostile environment in which you are forced to work, you are
not alone.

From the countless men and women who have poured out
their struggles and conflicts to me, I have learned a great deal
about what it means for a believer to endure a difficult work environment. Missed deadlines, petty supervisors, conflicts with
coworkers, overblown budgets, and frayed nerves become the
constant land mines waiting to detonate each day. Not only do
we experience the usual frustrations, office politics, and administrative red tape that every working person endures; as
Christians we often find our values clashing with those around
us, our faith conflicting with the office status quo. We often
find ourselves in the midst of a spiritual battlefield. We need to
know how to equip ourselves for the battle, how to prepare
ourselves for the fight, and how to balance our expectations
about what our job provides for us with our attitudes about
what we provide for our jobs. We need to let go of our "hire
power" and turn to the Higher Power of the Lord our God.
There's a "Help Wanted" sign on the front door of our workplace, and believers are the ones who need help in combat
survival.

Out of this need, I endeavor here to offer my humble ob-
servations and insights built around ten principles drawn from
God's Word concerning how we as His children should think

about, learn from, and live out His presence in our places of employment. Although I draw most of my examples from the way King David executed his job (which we'll get to shortly), I call these principles "ten commandments," for they remind me of the way the Lord revealed His laws for the well-being of the Children of Israel through Moses. While they wandered through the desert, even when they cast an idol in the form of a golden calf, God did not give up on His people. Instead, He provided for them, sending manna to feed them and dew to quench their thirst. To equip them spiritually for the temptations that lie along their journey like scorpions in the desert, God gave them His perfect law. He provided guidelines for their safety, success, and well-being. And while we often perceive the Ten Commandments as prohibitive and limiting, they really are just the opposite.

Have you ever watched a young child just beginning to walk? She totters this way and then zigzags the other way, weaving like a miniature adult who has indulged in too much wine. Or like a new colt, she may fall to her knees before picking herself up and continuing on her journey. But consider for a moment where that little girl would go if there were no adults around, if no doors, safety gates, fences, or windows contained her wobbly steps. She might well stagger into the neighbor's yard where the rottweiler has just gotten loose off his chain. She might scamper into the busy street, where the drivers of speeding SUVs would not see her in time to prevent injury. She might fall into a drainage ditch and be swept by the rain-bloated current washing down the gutter. No, it's vital that she have parameters so that she doesn't go too far and hurt herself. In fact, most children, as well as many adults, feel more freedom in knowing their limitations than in having limitless possibilities.

The Ten Commandments that Moses brought down from Mount Sinai were similar in their purpose and Divine intention. Because He created us in His image for relationship with Him, God knows best our limitations, just as a protective parent knows how to keep her toddler from wandering out into dangerous ground. Although delivered to the Israelites for their guidance, these Ten Commandments remain valid life instructions for us as His modern-day children. Instead of seeing them as a list of "thou shalt nots," we should seek out the Lord's intention of protection, guidance, and relationship with Him that they afford us. "Moses said to the people, 'Do not be afraid. God has come to test you, so that the fear of God will be with you to keep you from sinning' " (Exodus 20:20). God desires us to be happy and holy, and be sure— the two go together, for contentment and fulfillment can only be achieved when we walk straight along the path the Lord has set before us.

In a similar spirit, I offer you these ten commandments of working in a hostile environment. My hope is that you will be less afraid and more content, less concerned with job satisfaction and more centered on joyful expectancy regarding what the Source of your current position would have you do on the job. I hope that your frustrations will melt into a spirit of motivated purpose that will inspire those around you. When the hostilities increase, may your ability to solve problems and restore order, productivity, and creativity increase twice as much. These commandments are not a formula for success in your place of business, although you certainly may experience success as part of the blessings that He has for you when you're working within His plan. No, I intend these ten principles to serve as manna for your journey, nourishment and refreshment for your scorched soul as you struggle in your place of employment.

Even if you love your current job and don't work in a hostile environment, you can still learn how to better equip yourself for when conflict and trials do come around. And believe me, sooner or later they always come around! For the devil can't stand for God's people to advance His causes without a fight. So if your present workplace isn't hostile, then thank the Lord for this wonderful respite and use it to train yourself for when you will be sitting across the boardroom from a devil in disguise.

Please understand that I am certainly not a management expert, a corporate leadership consultant, or a motivational trainer—although I have performed all these roles in various endeavors. So I offer these commandments to you not as a prescriptive "you must do these or fail" type formula from Harvard Business School, but as a set of principles hard-won by experience and Divinely inspired so that I may serve to minister to those who desperately need guidance in the workplace.

Throughout the years, I have preached countless messages that have stirred me to the point of sleeplessness and unparalleled intensity. In the midst of even those, occasionally, one will surface that erupts like a volcano within me and catapults me to the pulpit, where I wait impatiently for the people to arrive and the music to end so that I can pour out the hot lava. The contents of this book came from one of those messages. I just know that you will change as a result of what God has so generously flowed from His throne to His own. You are going to find yourself in these pages and be challenged to rise to your true purpose and meaning in life regardless of what assaults you in your environment.

These ten principles can literally change your life. Now they may not change your boss, your coworkers, or the amount of overtime you have to work, but they can be used by God to change your attitude. For when you see that your Father is up to something, something for your ultimate good, it's easier to be at peace, to be joyful, to be patient as He uses your present circumstances—hostility and all—to bring about His plan and your destiny.

Throughout these pages, I am going to encourage you to drift away from what may seem like a mundane and meaningless life of countless e-mail and phone messages to a perspective that will cause you to lift your head and say, "I can't believe I've missed it. I'm on a mission here!" For you see, the greatest change and challenge we will ever effect is that of changing ourselves. Watch what happens around you when who you are—not what you say, what you preach, what you wear, or what you swear—rubs off and the life of Christ within you changes your world!

KNOW THAT
YOU ARE ANOINTED FOR
THE JOB OR POSITION
YOU NOW HOLD!

THE secretary gazes longingly at her boss's corner office, wondering why she's the one filing expense accounts and taking phone messages. The young realtor glances wistfully at his manager's high-volume award, wishing that he could sell as many properties with the same finesse and professionalism. A talented backup singer sways in the shadows, oohing and ahhing to the beat of the music, aching for the time when she will be the one in the spotlight singing lead.

It's so tempting to look at the lives of others and envy the fruit we see dangling across the fence in their backyard. Even if we enjoy our line of work, we may still think, "If only I had

Russell's job," or "If only I worked for the company where Sally works, then I'd be happy." Or even more tempting is to perceive another occupation or field as more fulfilling, more worthwhile, more lucrative, than our present one. "If only I hadn't wasted my time at this dead-end customer service job, then I could have started my own business." "If only I had gone to law school." "If only I had stayed with my band, we'd be at the top of the charts right now." On and on the "if only's" roll into a giant snowball, accumulating more and more discontent until finally you are blindsided and buried in a mound of depression and despair.

While it's human nature to think that the grass is always greener, I believe that it's one of the first areas where we must take control of our response to our present workplace. You may be thinking, "But Bishop Jakes, surely the Lord doesn't want me to be sweating for minimum wage?" or "Surely God doesn't intend for me to work in this prejudiced, unfair environment where unethical practices are the norm?"

My answer is that ultimately no, God wants much more for you than what your present workplace requires you to endure. The reality is that God often uses ordinary circumstances as a training ground to perfect our character. Furthermore, I have known Him to use some of the worst situations in my life to shine through me to others. Your presence in your current workplace may be so that you can be as a light in an otherwise dark and foreboding environment. Please indulge me a little history lesson as a way of clarifying this truth.

BACK TO THE FUTURE

There was a time in our country's history, traceable back to the European feudal systems with lords and barons and dukes and serfs, when the family into which you were born determined your social rank, economic position, level of attainable education, and lifetime's work. If you were born into a titled, aristocratic family then you might anticipate a life of leisure and educational pursuits. However, if your father was a blacksmith, then you would be expected to follow his trade and carry on the family business. And tragically enough, in this country if you were born into slavery, as many of our ancestors were, then you would likely be separated from your family and bound by the same forces that imprisoned your parents.

However, in the twentieth century, social and economic tides began to turn. New industrial plants emerged, unions were established, high technology was born, and the world was greatly altered by the onslaught of these developments. Pursuing the American dream meant that an individual—regardless of his country, family, or situation of origin—could work hard and work hard some more and achieve success.

African Americans also began to see changes—although at a slower pace. Sharecroppers moved up North and colored schools gave way to integration. The world began to take on a new perspective about race—a perspective that is still being formed in some regards. Admittedly, integration brought new hardships and a feeling of displacement for many; still, it helped to educate many of us who would have faced greater limitations today had it not occurred.

While freed of the social and economic inhibitors of past generations, this new burgeoning middle class comprised of whites, blacks, and a growing number of diverse cultural backgrounds often found themselves working for the same company for their entire lifetime. Craftsmen worked for the same construction company, assembly workers committed to the same manufacturer, teachers remained a constant presence at the same school year after year, and entry-level employees would gradually move into management and executive status with the major corporations. Nonetheless, they had the freedom to change careers, to improve their lot in life, like never before.

Enough of my little history lesson. Two reasons fuel my summation of hundreds of years of occupational history in a few dozen words. Foremost, I cover this ground to remind you of the foundation of sacrifices, prayers, hopes, and dreams that set the course you are presently pursuing. For many of us, our ancestors were hung in trees, beaten with whips, sprayed with water, and much worse as they fought to earn us the right to work for money rather than to be slaves who had to work for food. Where would we be without the mothers taking in laundry so that their children could take piano lessons, without the fathers working second jobs until they were too weary to stand, without the grandmothers and grandfathers working

tions inside out and establish Joseph as a leader to save a nation as well as his own family. On and on throughout the pages of His Word, God reveals story after story where disaster leads to destiny, where loss leads to laughter. There is a master plan unfolding in your life, and this job may only be a precursor to His finished design.

So before we embark further into our journey together to understand these principles I offer, I encourage you to look back upon the generational steps that have moved you in your present direction and to give thanks, trusting that God is redeeming your life to bring about His goodwill and your joy even as you are reading this page.

GOOD WORK

Part of our discontent often stems from the media image that a "successful" person doesn't need to work. While it's true that some independently wealthy folks don't have to work to earn an income upon which to live, they nonetheless have a job to do. You see, everyone is created for a Divine purpose, regardless of how much money is in their bank account.

Perhaps you have heard it preached or read in Scripture that work resulted from the fall of Adam and Eve in the garden when they ate the forbidden fruit. God tells Adam, "Cursed is the ground for your sake; in toil you shall eat of it all the days of your life. In the sweat of your face you shall eat bread . . ."

(Genesis 3:17, 19). While it's true that work took on a different meaning after the fall, it's a mistake to believe that our first parents were without purpose prior to this incident.

From the time that Adam and Eve were created, it's been clear that God intended for us to be just like our Creator, productive, fruitful, and invested in tasks contributing to His purposes. They were given reign over the garden and enjoyed a maximum level of fulfillment in their jobs before their selfish decision to disobey.

> Then the Lord God took the man and put him in the garden of Eden to tend and to keep it. Out of the ground the Lord God formed every beast of the field and every bird of the air; and brought them to Adam to see what he would call them. And whatever Adam called each living creature, that was its name.
>
> (GENESIS 2:15, 19)

The first job description included tending, keeping, and naming—the ultimate manager's position! Similarly, Eve was created to share in these endeavors as Adam's helper. A man who wasn't busy wouldn't need a helper. So we need look no further than the first pages of the first book of the Bible to realize that work is not all about suffering, toiling, and sweating.

RIGHT MAN FOR THE JOB

Perhaps a better picture of a person living out his purpose emerges from one of the most dynamic figures in all of Scripture. God uses David to teach so many truths, but it seems almost inconceivable that a man who never wore a dress suit, pushed a broom, or carried a briefcase might be our biblical model for this subject. However, let's take a look at a passage of Scripture from I Samuel 16 and watch how the Old Testament hero and model of grace once again plays the part God wants to highlight: His perfect employee.

And he sent, and brought him in. Now he was ruddy, and withal of a beautiful countenance, and goodly to look to. And the LORD said, Arise, anoint him: for this is he.

Then Samuel took the horn of oil, and anointed him in the midst of his brethren: and the Spirit of the LORD came upon David from that day forward. So Samuel rose up, and went to Ramah.

But the Spirit of the LORD departed from Saul, and an evil spirit from the LORD troubled him.

And Saul's servants said unto him, Behold now, an evil spirit from God troubleth thee.

Let our lord now command thy servants, which are before thee, to seek out a man, who is a cunning player on a harp: and it shall come to pass, when the evil spirit from

God is upon thee, that he shall play with his hand, and thou shalt be well.

And Saul said unto his servants, Provide me now a man that can play well, and bring him to me.

Then answered one of the servants, and said, Behold, I have seen a son of Jesse the Bethlehemite, that is cunning in playing, and a mighty valiant man, and a man of war, and prudent in matters, and a comely person, and the LORD is with him.

Wherefore Saul sent messengers unto Jesse, and said, Send me David thy son, which is with the sheep.

And Jesse took an ass laden with bread, and a bottle of wine, and a kid, and sent them by David his son unto Saul.

And David came to Saul, and stood before him: and he loved him greatly; and he became his armourbearer.

And Saul sent to Jesse, saying, Let David, I pray thee, stand before me; for he hath found favour in my sight.

And it came to pass, when the evil spirit from God was upon Saul, that David took a harp, and played with his hand: so Saul was refreshed, and was well, and the evil spirit departed from him.

(I SAMUEL 16:12–23, KJV)

While a young shepherd boy was receiving his first anointing, which would eventually result in his becoming king, we find the king being harassed by an evil spirit. The critical timing of these two incidents reveals the hand of God in each and the plan of God to anoint this young man to enter a hostile environment. It is of notable interest for us that David is already God's chosen even though someone else is occupying his space. At only age fifteen, David is about to become equipped for his destiny, which begins with simply playing a harp for the troubled king. David, who would be king, begins his journey to greatness by being faithful to what might have seemed to some mediocre and mundane. Yet God often prepares us for greatness by teaching us faithfulness in a substandard situation. It doesn't matter where you start. It only matters where you finish!

Two other truths leap out at me from across these pages of Scripture. The first is simply the fact that David was anointed prior to filling the position where his talents were most needed. He didn't have to prove himself first and "win" the position the way we often do as we compete for jobs against other well qualified candidates. I know he was well qualified, but what I am saying is that David was anointed for something beyond what he was appointed to do at that time. Also, his anointing from God has to do with his character qualifications, not necessarily his job skills—although these are important too. For sure, if David couldn't play the harp or create the beautiful lyrics that we find in the Psalms, then he wouldn't have gotten this job in the first place. However, it is his integrity, passion, and commitment to serving God that allows him to keep the position. Basically, David's resumé was complete—he "is cunning in playing, and a mighty valiant man, and a man of war, and prudent in matters, and a comely person, and the LORD is with him." He had it all goin' on! A talented musician, a brave soldier, mature, poised, attractive, and filled with the Lord's presence. We should all be so blessed!

And the truth is that we *are* all this blessed. We may not have these particular attributes, but like a snowflake, a fingerprint, no two people are alike; we all have our own mix of gifts and talents, abilities and creativities. Just as the Lord recognized and anointed David, so He charts our growth and knows when we are ready to fill the spot that He has prepared for us.

Which brings us to the second truth that is so striking here. David's contribution complements the need of his new workplace. While David is young, vital, peaceful, brave, attractive, and filled with God's presence, his new boss is old, weary, anxious, afraid, insecure, and troubled by an evil spirit. So often we are tempted to seek out jobs with others who have the same background, education, and skill set as our own. However, it's likely that we may be most needed in the places where there's a void in our areas of giftedness and expertise. We may not like this environment or feel as comfortable as we would in a more homogenous, conformist workplace, but we wouldn't be needed there nearly as much. We must learn to see beyond our own comfort zone and into the jobs where we may be most needed.

THE POWER OF POSITIVE PURPOSE

We were once just a thought in our Father's mind, and He strategically arranged the details of our lives—just as He did David's—to enter earth right on time to be precisely where He needed us to be. We have only one life to give back to the Master, and where we serve is His call. The workplace—wherever yours is—consumes countless hours of our lives. It behooves us all at this point to measure the parameters of our "work lives" not by our own instruments but by the same hand that spans the heavens. He has a plan. A plan that we can't always see or appreciate in the moment.

Notice that the Bible says that an evil spirit came upon Saul, but it doesn't say that God is an evil spirit. When evil comes your way, be comforted knowing that God is in control. He monitors how much evil we have. When the enemy has come in like a flood, God will raise up a standard. Enough is enough, devil! We can sense that the devil is in that fire, but we can rest assured that God has His hand on the thermostat! Job tells us that the devil has to be given permission to attack us; so if God is allowing an attack, He is planning on our victory! God would not want us to be in a battle we could not win! I know it can be challenging to perceive this when you are in the midst of a crisis or conflict. If you aren't able to have that perspective right now, ask your Father to grant you opportuniti- where you might grow and trust Him more.

It seems likely that such a prayer may have been difficult for Saul to pray. The present king wanted to protect his position and his peace of mind more than he wanted to know the Lord. In this particular passage of Scripture, we are told that the Spirit of the Lord departed from Saul and an evil spirit entered. God was simply using the evil to set the stage for His chosen people. God looks for and finds some handpicked, chosen people to enter an evil environment so that He might be glorified. God's plan is to make it work for good. So don't be intimidated by the devil; just keep vigilant to see what God is up to!

God strategically sends people into hostile environments that they might bring about the change that He desires. It is an honor to be chosen by God and sent into a hostile environment. I know these situations can be uncomfortable, but when it's all over God will be glorified and the one sent will be blessed! Just focus on this: God is not as interested in your comfort as He is in your purpose. Equate it to physical exercise; regardless of the newfangled exercise gadgets that let you "work out" while you sit at the computer, the truth remains: no pain, no gain. No effort, no reward. Jesus was able to endure much hardship because His focus was on purpose, not pleasure and momentary gain. God knows that if we become too comfortable in any given position, we will just lounge there too long basking in peace and nonconfrontational bliss and miss out on the real blessings that come through focus, warfare, and determination.

Somehow we, as a church, have not prepared Christians for the warfare that is required for winning. Or the attitude that characterizes a champion. I realize that an image of a soldier seems a little rigid for a believer, but we are told to "endure hardship as a good soldier." We need to be taught and trained that life as a Christian involves various kinds of warfare, and one of those is often to go right into the midst of the heated battle. That's why God sends His people into deplorable work settings. So easily we get caught up in mundane, unimportant things in life and neglect our real responsibility on earth: to bring God everywhere we go. High-ranking military officials spend tremendous hours poring over maps and determining areas to send troops. That kind of strategy parallels our Christian warfare. New Testament radical believers were willing to march into enemy territory and suffer beyond our imagination to further the spread of Christianity. Are we that kind of Christian?

In this story about Saul and David, God had a plan in motion. While David was out in the pasture tending sheep, everyone's eyes were on Saul. Meanwhile, God had His eye on David, watching how he worshipped, how his character was coming along, his relationship with and fear of God, and how he confronted evil. Was he easily intimidated or did he have the stuff kings are made of? How would he fare in battle? Would he see a giant or a giant God standing behind him with all power and might? Was he arrogant, proud, and self-sufficient, running ahead of God before seeking battle plans, or did he rely solely on God? Would he be fair with people? How would he handle authority? Would he speak evil of those placed over him, or would he recognize their position and know that God's requirement included that those in authority be given respect and honor?

David wasn't aware what God had planned for him, but he acknowledged God in all his ways and is referred to as a "man after God's own heart." Someone once said that "character is what you are when nobody is watching." Well, God is always watching. He was watching David and He is watching you. Most Christians do not work as though God is watching them or even cares about the job they are doing. They fail to realize that promotion doesn't come "from the east or the west . . . but from God" (Psalm 75:6–7).

Saul was not God's chosen instrument. He was not God's choice for the job. God was orchestrating the divine stage for His chosen people and for Himself to be glorified. David was chosen and David was the "man for the job."

The truth is, we are all chosen. There are roughly six billion people in the world, and God keeps perfect track of each and every one of us. Your whereabouts are clear and current with Him. And be assured, He always has an absolutely strategic assignment for you. Sometimes you may not appreciate your current situation; it may be difficult and unpleasant. But know that God has seeded the assignment for a full future harvest of blessings. David understood the hand of God, so when he found himself on his "assignment," David entertained the enemy with the melodious sounds of praise. If you have been

placed in a hostile environment, keep in mind that God deliberately deposited you there and you too can appease the
enemy while you are being trained for future greatness.

Can you not feel the elevation in your spirit as you shift
your focus from one of victimization to one of being chosen?
Surely God would only send those He could trust into a "military zone." God cares about where you are and has selected
your work environment. It may change from time to time, but
it's His choice for you that matters. Pause to reflect on the fact
that with God there are no insignificant, random maneuvers. If
He chose you, He has already or is currently equipping you.
You can count on that! You wouldn't send your child off to
camp without his bags being completely packed or making
provision in some way for everything he would need while
away. Now if we, earthly parents, know how to give good gifts
to our children, how much more can our Heavenly Father give
us? God has a plan so great for you that your finite mind cannot comprehend the full scope.

I know that sometimes hostile environments can be over-
whelming and seem too much to bear. But we can survive them.
If God's people will take God to work and keep their identity
intact, the enemy will lose ground. The enemy knows this, and
so he keeps the believer focusing on absolutely everything that
is problematic. He makes us focus on the gossip, on the office
politics, on the too-heavy workload, the too-low pay, the mi-
cromanaging supervisor and the injustice of a system that
seems to promote based more on who you know than what yo

do. So there the believer is with blankets of despair weighing him down while the enemy sneers with delight.

The danger is that we focus on the discomfort of the moment and miss the miracles that lie beyond the season. We're so distraught that we cry out to our Lord to deliver us from our misery, but while we are praying for God to change conditions and take away the discomfort, He is saying, "Oh, child, if only you knew what awaited you. Your purpose and destiny are only moments away and, though not wrapped in shiny paper, contain all you will ever need to reach your purpose and bring Me glory." God understands us so perfectly that He realizes our tendency to stay too long if things are comfortable, thus, He often has to trouble the water so that we will reach out to Him in desperation for the strength that is made perfect in our weakness.

TROUBLESHOOTING

David did not attempt to pray away his problem. If David had prayed away Saul's evil spirit, he also would have prayed away his opportunity to serve God in that environment and the ones to follow. David knew God was up to something good, so he kept his joy, tuned his ear to God, and found out what the moment demanded in order for God to show up. God is a troubleshooter, so when He sees trouble, He sends a shooter. He knew what the stituation needed and He sent in the right person—David—to do what needed to be done. Oh, brothers and sisters, get ahold of this for yourselves! God sees your gifts and talents and launches you right into those spots where they shine like lasers in the night! Where better to be bright than in darkness? Where better to utilize your gifts than in an insipid, fruitless environment? God can empower you, just as He did David, to be the solution to the problem—whatever it is—so that God can be God right in the midst of the mess!

Another thing to note is that when David was called, he didn't just come; he came with gifts. When he was told he was going to stand before Saul, he didn't ask "why?" or "what's in this for me?" No, David went freely and he brought with him food, wine, a young goat, and his harp-playing skills. Biblical protocol demanded that the visitor bring a gift to the blessed or gifted man, and David brought his gifts. There is so much to be learned from that lesson. Too many people are overly concerned with what they can receive rather than what they can give. We need to break that "gimme spirit" and replace it with a heart that comes to serve. When that attitude is in operation we can focus on being all that we can be—all that God created us to be. Think not about the problems but what you can achieve in the midst of the problems. Grab ahold of David's example and pray for God to show you what problem you have been assigned to attack. And do it with the right spirit. In order to do what God has for us to do, we must use what God has given us to use.

Keeping a right attitude will serve you all the days of your life. A right attitude and faith will allow you to say, "This may be a hard time, baby, but it's also short-term. My Father is busy even now preparing a better position for me or even creating one if one does not exist. Therefore, I will not complain. I will check my attitude and be grateful for what I have so that I can be trusted in what I am about to be given. While I am here, I will make God happy that He picked me for the job and show those I work for that they need what I've got!"

DRESS FOR SUCCESS

Before we go any further, we need to take a long and serious look at a fundamental issue. It sounds simple, but it is a loaded question: Are you a Christian? "Christ" is not Jesus's last name. "Christ" is descriptive of what He was anointed to do: save the people from their sins. In other words, He was anointed to carry out that redemption. David was anointed in his house to be effective on his job. And you too are anointed for a specific assignment. Being anointed means you are fully armed and equipped to do the job you are meant to do.

Every profession has its own requirements, specific tools, and uniforms necessary for optimal performance. If we work on telephone poles, there's a whole suit of clothing and protective devices for that line of work; if we work with poisons or hazardous substances, proper dress is provided for precaution against contamination of our bodies. Whether it's the doctors in surgical scrubs or firefighters in heat-resistant uniforms, proper attire is required to carry out the job. As Christians, we also have to dress for work. No, we don't necessarily need to fuss with our outward appearance (although dressing for success is a smart tactic, for how we're perceived can go a long way toward helping us achieve), but we must dress up our character and spirit by "putting on the Lord Jesus Christ." We are representatives of God, commissioned to build up His Kingdom. We must drape ourselves in His glory and let our actions indicate that we are on this job carrying out the orders of our Lord.

The world is totally confused about who Christians are, and these misconceptions are continually fed by our inability to step out in our true colors and show up for what we really believe. Your workplace doesn't need a sermon; they could get that on television. Your job, however, is your pulpit. How you conduct yourself should reflect what you believe and serve as a testimony to God's will.

Some may protest that it's difficult to maintain Christian integrity when you have to deal with backstabbing, corporate sabotage, unethical management, and the misuse of power. How can you stand firm when the enemy is all around you trying to cut you down? Actually, we Christians are at our best when the enemy comes. The anointing is activated by enemy encroachment. As situations get worse, God will increase the anointing. Sometimes we have to ge more creative as challenges enlarge or intensify. Someti

you may have to step outside of the situation and remind
yourself Who put you there. Leave your office, take a break,
or simply go to the restroom and call on your Boss. God is
very present in times of trouble, and learning to call on Him
instead of falling into the trap of the enemy is what wins
wars! When adversity and challenge come—and surely they
will come—remember this:

"I can do all things through Christ who strengthens me!"
(PHILIPPIANS 4:13)

Remember that God purposely placed you right where you
are. You may experience budget cuts, financial trouble, layoffs,
or communication problems on your job. But God sent you
there with an anointing to get the job done. He has a reason
for His maneuver and you have a purpose for your life.

Stop perceiving challenges as problems and consider them
stepping-stones for success. God has chosen you. He has
anointed you. Anointing is the empowerment by God to do
what only God can do through us. His power is at work inside
of you. When you feel overwhelmed or underappreciated, dis-
gusted and dissatisfied with your current job, just remember
that God has a divine plan for you and with His power at work
in you, you can persevere.

MARCHING ORDERS

The workplace where you have been called is your assignment. Sure it may be a hard place, but you are there for a reason. You have been honored with an assignment that will bring Him glory. God is using a mighty tool—you! If you're in a dark place, be the light and love the privilege! Use the example of David's life to glean insight into how Christians should face their challenges. Go back and read those verses and think about David's perspective, his approaches, his attitude, and the way he lived his life. If you are going to step into the role God has ordained for you, you need to embrace your current situation.

There is a reason you are right where you are; God put you there. Along comes the enemy and sticks thorns in God's children so that they will squirm away from the designated assignment, become overwhelmed, and go AWOL! Don't let him win!

Encourage yourself in the Lord by praying, "I am the woman for the job! I am the man for the job! Nobody else could do this job, Lord, so you gave it to me. Nobody else could handle the responsibilities You have set before me. I am trusting You to bring treasure out of this trash, to turn my life around and deliver me from the bondage of the enemy! Lord, you have never failed me; now I will not fail you. I will trust in your anointing, God, and bring you glory out of all these failures. I am not expecting the enemy to like me, so I am reminding myself of who I am and whose I am. I AM THE PERSON FOR THE JOB! Help me, Lord, to be found faithful and to hear You say in the end, 'Well done, good and faithful servant!'"

DON'T EXPECT TO BE APPRECIATED

MANY people complain that their job doesn't satisfy them because no one in their workplace appreciates what they contribute. They say things like, "If my supervisor only realized how much I give to this team . . ." or "I wish my coworkers would acknowledge my contribution . . ." and "It would be nice to get a little credit for all that I do." While I understand the innate craving to be recognized, appreciated, and valued for what we do, I'm afraid these folks are in for a rather rude awakening. You see, when this desire becomes the condition upon which their contentment rests, then they have bought into a falsehood that can threaten to keep them in a place of misery.

Our workplace is not the place to be affirmed. If we go back to David, we'll see that he was affirmed at home, not in his new place of employment. He was anointed before he ever got to the king's palace. This enabled him to serve, to give, to provide his skills for his new boss, the king, rather than expecting Saul to provide for his needs. No, David's fundamental need to know who he was and what God had in store for him had already been established. This youngest of many brothers, overlooked by his own father while he herded sheep out in the hills, had been chosen by God.

Now, in my thinking, if anyone had reason to go into a job with some major expectations, it's someone like David, whom God has anointed as the next king of His people. If you or I were walking in David's sandals, it would be oh-so-tempting to demand respect and subservience from those in the palace where we would soon rule.

However, this is not what this man after God's own heart displays in his first official job as harp player and attendant to King Saul. We see humility, excellence in his skillfulness, and an attitude of service and loyalty despite the hostility in his new environment. And if playing music to soothe the most powerful man at the time, who just happened to be afflicted by troubling demons, isn't a position of pressure, then I'm not sure what is.

Too often we justify our complaints and our plans and schemes to be recognized and appreciated in our workplace. We may be thinking, "No one else is going to do it for me, so

I better make sure I'm valued for who I know I am." I understand this feeling. Anyone who has worked in any kind of job for more than a few days can empathize. But when we fall into this ego trap, led by our pride and fear, we forget that God knows what we have to offer. He knows what we have to contribute because He placed it there within us. While we may not be patted on the back at the weekly staff meeting or recognized in the company newsletter as employee of the month, God will reveal Himself through us if we will only allow Him to shine through our diligent work. It's often an act of faith and deliberate obedience to step out of the spotlight and work behind the scenes.

SECRET IDENTITY

By comparison to what we encounter on the job, superheroes have it easy. They know that beneath their business suit there's a uniform with its accompanying emblem that reflects who they really are—whether it's the big red S of Superman, the black bat of Batman, or the triumphant eagle of Wonder Woman. These characters all humbly endure their jobs' requirements in order to avoid drawing attention to themselves. Clark Kent doesn't want his boss and coworkers suspecting the real strength, power, and ability lurking below his mild-mannered persona. His superpowers do not come from his work environment, from the adulation and recognition afforded him by his job. No, his superpowers are inside him, waiting to be displayed at the necessary time, all while he goes about his job as a reporter.

Forgetting our own true identity is one of the easiest ways to set ourselves up for failure in the workplace. If we forget who we really are and begin to think that our job defines us, then we're in for a bumpy ride as we rise and fall with the opinion of others around us. Taken to an extreme, we become ineffectual because we're not willing to make decisions or to take risks of our own, for fear that they might negatively affect what others think of us. We become a "yes man" or "yes woman" who nods and agrees like some bobblehead doll on the receptionist's desk, agreeing with anyone and everyone just to please them and have them like us. Consequently, our value to the company plummets because we don't utilize our God-given gifts and we offer no contribution to the company.

We must keep in mind that who we are is not based on what we do in the workplace. Our identity does not revolve around the title after our name, the size of our office, or whether we were named employee of the month on the shiny plaque in the reception area. Being an attorney, a baker, a custodian, an electrician, a foreman, a businesswoman, a pilot, or a manager is only a small part of who we are, only a spoke radiating from the center of our identity as a son or daughter of the King, not the hub turning the wheel.

But consider how often we make our profession our possession, our badge that we flash at the world to identify who we are and what we're about. When meeting someone for the first time, and they ask, "Who are you?" it can be tempting to say, "I'm Freddy and I'm a stockbroker." Now there's nothing wrong with selling stocks, but there's so much more to Freddy and so much more inside the complex layers of our identity than we can ever sum up in giving our occupation.

I'll never forget the delightful response of a dear older sister in a church I once pastored. Whenever anyone would ask her who she was or what she did, she would beam her big pearly smile back at them and say, "I'm Charlene and I'm full-time blessed." This woman had realized that her identity as God's child, as a woman created in her Creator's image, as a follower of her Savior Jesus Christ, was at the core of who she was and the blessing she was living out. The fact that she also had worked as a dressmaker, hairstylist, caterer, day care worker, teacher, and retailer were not part of her core identity.

Knowing who we are apart from what we do is as essential to our success in the workplace as our credentials and skill set. Otherwise, we will compromise and lose sight of what we are on the job to do and instead look for every opportunity to be recognized, to be a "showboat," to grab the spotlight, and to be the center of attention. We end up working harder at being appreciated than at whatever our job happens to be!

This not only sends the wrong signal to our coworkers and supervisors, it robs us of our true identity in Christ and the solid foundation of security, peacefulness, and joy that it provides. Instead, our self-worth fluctuates like a politician's popularity in an election year, up one day and down the next. We end up riding a roller coaster of moodiness and unexpected disappointments alongside a few moments of praise, which may or may not be sincere, for once others learn that we thrive on recognition they then hold the key to manipulating us to suit their own purposes.

TALENT SHOW

And this is another problem with thirsting after appreciation on the job. It gives others such power over us, power to define us and to influence our self-worth. We become people pleasers and not God pleasers. It's awfully hard to hear God's voice, often directing us against the tide of popular opinion, when we have tuned our ears to only respond to the boss's voice, the team leader's assessment, or the customer's remarks. In His Word, God frequently reminds us that we are to seek Him first rather than the approval of others. "Therefore, whether you eat or drink, or whatever you do, do all to the glory of God" (1 Corinthians 10:31).

Whether you're pushing a broom across an elementary school floor or planning a million-dollar budget for your company's next fiscal year, you should do it as unto the Lord. For His glory. Not for your own. Not even for your employer's glory. But for God's and His alone. When you experience His pleasure in what you're doing, even if it's something you hate doing but know that it's where you should be at the present moment, then you won't need the affirmation from your coworkers.

One way to keep this as our compass on the job is to make sure that we're focused on the "true North" of what God values, not what will make us most prominent in the corporate show-case. And what does God value in our job performance? In Scripture we're reminded that He values humility and servant-hood, not pride and entitlement. "Humble yourselves in the sight of the Lord, and He will lift you up" (James 4:10). If we are secure in our identity as His son or daughter, then we can relax and know that like the loving parent He is, our God will recognize His own and reward us justly and graciously. We know what a privilege it is to be His creation, a masterpiece in progress, and such truth frees us from having to be recognized by others and praised by men and women.

God also values courage and risk taking. Consider what faith it took for David to leave his home, the earthy, smelly shepherd's pallet on the hillsides, and travel to the royal palace. He must have felt just a little out of place, knowing that he was underdressed and uninformed about the culture and customs of the royal court. Like a boy from the projects suddenly finding himself in the White House, David was instantly out of his comfort zone! And then later, after it's clear that his new boss is afflicted by an evil spirit and intends to kill him, David coolly maintains his mission because he knows that God wants him there.

Or consider another powerful example of how our Father values risk taking. In telling the parable of the talents, Jesus makes it vividly clear that we are not to bury our talents but to multiply them. Reflect on this passage with me for a moment:

For the kingdom of heaven is like a man traveling to a far country, who called his own servants and delivered his goods to them. And to one he gave five talents, to another two, and to another one, to each according to his own ability; and immediately he went on a journey. Then he who had received the five talents went and traded with them, and made another five talents. And likewise he who had received two gained two more also. But he who had received one went and dug in the ground, and hid his lord's money. After a long time the lord of those servants came and settled accounts with them.

So he who had received five talents came and brought five other talents, saying, "Lord, you delivered to me five talents; look, I have gained five more talents besides them." His lord said to him, "Well done, good and faithful servant; you were faithful over a few things, I will make you ruler over many things. Enter into the joy of your lord." He also who had received two talents came and said, "Lord, you delivered to me two talents; look, I have gained two more talents besides them." His lord said to him, "Well done, good and faithful servant; you have been faithful over a few things, I will make you ruler over many things. Enter into the joy of your lord."

Then he who had received the one talent came and said, "Lord, I knew you to be a hard man, reaping where you have not sown, and gathering where you have not scattered seed. And I was afraid, and went and hid your talent in the ground. Look, there you have what is yours."

But his lord answered and said to him, "You wicked and lazy servant, you knew that I reap where I have not sown, and gather where I have not scattered seed. So you ought to have deposited my money with the bankers, and at my coming I would have received back my own with interest. Therefore take the talent from him, and give it to him who has ten talents.

"For to everyone who has, more will be given, and he will have abundance; but from him who does not have, even what he has will be taken away. And cast the unprofitable servant into the outer darkness. There will be weeping and gnashing of teeth."

(MATTHEW 25:14–30)

Can there be any more powerful incentive for godly risk taking than we see demonstrated in this parable? Ultimately, don't we want our performance review to be from our Master and not our supervisor? The richest, most fulfilling affirmation we can experience is hearing our Lord say to us, "Well done, good and faithful servant. Enter into the joy of the Lord." And surely the most horrific criticism is leveled at the wicked servant who was too afraid to take a chance, or even to use common sense and deposit his talent in a conservative, safe place where it would still turn a profit. It seems clear that in the outer darkness to which this servant is cast, his own anger, sorrow, and regret are his only reward, not the favor of the Lord.

FAIL-SAFE

Several other items command our attention in this parable. It's striking that the servant who worried most about pleasing his master is the one who took no risk whatsoever. This servant made the mission all about his own performance rather than the actual mission of making the most of what he'd been given as a good steward. This can be difficult to keep in mind, but we must realize that good stewardship requires risk taking. Certainly not the reckless, selfish, careless risk taking that loses sight of the goal in shortsighted fashion. No, good stewardship requires that we boldly and courageously exercise faith as we plant the seeds that we've been given in the soil of our workplace. We can risk failure because our worth does not depend on our external success. If we are doing our best and striving to live out God's calling, and we appear to fail in our endeavors, then we must realize that God is training us for later success. We must view our failures and shortcomings not as deficiencies but as lessons.

Failure can actually teach us so much about what we need to change as we move forward and attempt our next venture. And we must remember that we have a security net beneath us that allows us to fail safely. God will never let us fall. However, if our identity and self-worth is all tied up in knots around the failed enterprise, then we will not be motivated to try again. After all, who wants to feel like a failure over and over again? It's human nature to want to feel good, to succeed, to win the prize, to move forward and not backward. But like a world-class athlete backing up so that he can run faster, jump higher, or throw farther, we must accept that a few backward steps now can fuel our forward progress later.

We must also keep in mind that our Father assesses our accomplishments differently than those around us. What appears to be failure in the eyes of men is often a Divine success in the eyes of God. Certainly the most striking example of this emerges in the sacrifice of His Son—sending Him to earth so that He could become the gateway for us to enter heaven. Throughout the life of Christ, it seems that He and His Father made it clear that things are not always what they appear to be from a human perspective. Instead of a royal prince born in splendor, like the Three Kings expected (along with Herod), Jesus was born into the most humble of nurseries—a feeding trough in a dusty barn surrounded by animals and shepherds. Instead of an earthly kingdom involving armies, palaces, treasures, and manpower, Jesus established a heavenly Kingdom centered on doing His Father's will. And instead of a coronation of political pageantry, Jesus established our salvation by His execution on two beams of rough-hewn wood, nails penetrating His flesh as He suffered alongside two common criminals even as the crowds jeered and laughed. Even His disciples thought that Jesus had been defeated, that God's plan had failed. As eyewitnesses to their Master's humiliating death, they could not imagine what was about to happen: Jesus rising from the dead, throwing off His grave clothes, and demonstrating His deity with a power and majesty that this world had never seen.

So often our inability to imagine God's purpose to redeem our perceived failures limits us from receiving His ultimate blessings. When Joseph's brothers sold him into slavery, they acted out of envy, spite, and hatred. But their actions were used by God to bring about their survival as well as the survival of millions of others. For if they hadn't sold Joseph, he would have never made it to Pharaoh and would have never been around to save Egypt from famine. As Joseph explained to his brothers, "You intended to harm me, but God intended it for good to accomplish what is now being done, the saving of many lives" (Genesis 50:20, NIV). We must be willing to risk, and to fail, and trust that God is up to something that requires us transcending what we can imagine. This process is so much easier if we are not bound up in equating such failures with our identities.

DON'T TAKE IT PERSONALLY

A job should not be the source of your affirmation. Get that clear in your mind and maybe get yourself a little desk rock that reminds you why you are there and why you are not. Now if you get appreciated or affirmed, wonderful. But I can promise you that if being appreciated is your sole reason for performing and working, God will have people overlook you until you get the order of work straight in your mind. You can get appreciated at home, by your friends, your family, or your volunteer group at the hospital, but work is just what it sounds like: work. You are on that job to give and to give and to give some more. A job is not a personal environment. It is a professional environment. Don't let that job affect who you are; you are sent to bring in godliness, not get gratification for personal needs.

One of the absolutely surest ways to become disappointed is to make our expectations so unrealistic that we are continually depressed. Too-high expectations lead to frustrations. Spouses set them up for marriages; parents for children, children for parents; church folk for pastors, pastors for church folk; people for jobs. A job should not be your identity. It should be an environment for you to exercise your gifts. You are not your job. Your identity is a child of God, placed on an assignment that can change at any given moment according to what the Father has planned.

Letting that job grip you personally can lead to pitfalls. If you are on a challenging mission right at this moment, check to see if your thoughts include what someone thinks of you, what people are saying about you, and on and on. . . . Don't get all caught up in "Why didn't they recognize me? *I* should have been employee of the month." "Well, why did *he* get a raise?"

Sometimes we just get too caught up in people. Stay hooked up with your Source who gave you the job, who will give you the raise, and who will always be there to affirm you.

Jesus sprang up like a root in dry ground. Talk about a tough situation. God dressed up in a man's body and went to earth to live among people who wanted to kill Him because He wanted to save them. He left every amenity of heaven—which we are hard-pressed to even imagine—to enter earth, an un-friendly, hostile environment filled with thieves, betrayers, re-ligious stiff-necks, and the devil face-to-face. He pulled away a lot. Go through the New Testament and discover what a con-secrated, set-apart life He had to live in order to live amidst His very own, who despised, rejected, and finally crucified Him. He spent much time in prayer and came back from visits with His Father encouraged and empowered. Jesus kept one thing on His mind: He came to do the will of His Father. And He told us that as the Father had sent Him, so sent He us! So we, too, should keep our Father's will in mind as we endeavor to survive our struggles. We need to remember that He sent us, and we have a job to do.

When we know that we are not our own, that our well-being and identity are not dependent upon the recognition of others, then we can experience a level of peace, joy, and con-tentment even in the harshest of work environments. When we know that God appreciates us, then we can have a healthy self-confidence, not a weak, dependent character that needs prop-ping up like a loose signpost by everyone who comes along.

———◆———

EMBRACE OPPORTUNITIES
FOR CHANGE

ONE of the greatest sources of friction in many people's work environment is change. Just when you get on solid ground with your manager, she's promoted and you have to learn to relate to her successor. Just when you complete that big project and look forward to some downtime, a new and bigger account takes its place. Just when you thought you had the office politics figured out, your company is bought out by another corporation. And on and on the cycle of change spins, leaving us dazed and unsettled by its turbulence.

Much of this friction is caused by our expectations and our

desire for things to go smoothly. It is indeed ironic that out of our desire for stability, security, and predictability we set ourselves up for instability, uncertainty, and surprises. Perhaps if we adjusted our expectations to be more realistic, we wouldn't be so traumatized when change comes. And rest assured—it will come. We should expect change in our workplace and know that only God can serve as our secure anchor, our unshakable, immovable rock.

So often we view job security as the be-all and end-all, the condition upon which we can finally rest and coast through our remaining time in the workplace. Once we become used to the personalities of our coworkers or team members, we want them to remain in place, stay the same, and require nothing more out of us than what we've given in the past. *Even when our work environment is hostile, as long as it's predictable, many people grow accustomed to it and lose sight of their purpose for being there.* You may even realize that much of your job dissatisfaction stems from boredom, from being stuck in a rut, locked inside the box instead of having the freedom to risk thinking outside it. But nonetheless, you know what to expect and would rather be bored and stifled from reaching your full potential than face the discomforting dynamics of change.

You don't have to work very long—or live that long, for that matter—to realize that change is inevitable. It's part of the reality of life, part of God's plan, part of the dynamic design of His creation. Yet why are we so resistant to embracing change? Why does change in our workplace threaten us in particular?

Let's unpack some of the reasons and work at understanding how we can view change, especially in our workplace, as opportunities for growth and maturity.

FOUR SEASONS

As I've experienced and observed the process of spiritual maturation, I've noticed that there are at least four stages regarding expectations, which I compare to the four seasons. We begin as new Christians in the spring. Many of us came out of crises and life-changing experiences—brutal storms in our lives—and God intervened and lifted us out of the miry clay and set us upon His firm rock. Change occurs all around us and produces beautiful results. Flowers are blooming out of nowhere, our cold heart has melted, and life is a new reality where once we hoped for little. Our life turnaround is so dramatic, so beyond anything we ever expected, that we are stunned by the wonder of it all.

However, eventually the dramatic storm of our conversion becomes a steady falling rain that soon tapers off, producing a rainbow in a bright summer sky. Life drifts into predictable patterns and rhythms. Slowly we sink back into expecting things to remain the same, secure and comfortable. We begin to fear anything that threatens our status quo as we focus on remaining at ease and in control. But sooner or later, a hurricane of change comes whirling into our safe little summer resort, forc-

nge whether we like it or not. It may be the
:tting downsized from our job, or being di-
e-altering illness. If we live long enough in
l experience the unexpected. A flash flood of
tragic propo... is will catch us off guard, and we become
frightened, angry, and unsettled when these storms hit us. We
may likely wonder why God would allow such a storm to en-
velop our lives, why our peace would be disrupted.

As the floodwaters subside and stability returns, we enter
the autumn season of change, the uncertainty of life causing us
to be timid and insecure. We crave stability and tranquility, the
security of knowing what will happen, when it will happen,
and what will be required of us in the meantime. But we worry
and fret, knowing that nothing is as stable as we would like it
to be. We are aware that life can turn on a dime. We can wake
up tomorrow and find out a loved one has cancer, be told that
our services are no longer needed on the job, or discover that
our spouse is in love with someone else. We don't know what's
coming, we only know that change will come.

Which brings us to the final stage of how we manage
change—the winter season. We finally realize, like the
preacher in Ecclesiastes, that everything changes all the time,
even as it stays the same. Change is the only constant in life.
"To everything there is a season, a time for every purpose under
heaven," he writes, including as his refrain that "all is vanity and
grasping for the wind" (Ecclesiastes 3:1; 2:17). Our awareness
of life's fragility and frailty leads us to cling to God as our only

immutable, unchangeable, permanent fixture in our lives. Winter brings cold and snow, ice and rain, but we learn to see the beauty of even the harshest storm and cling to the fire where He burns in our hearts. We expect change and embrace it as a way of knowing God more intimately.

David reaches this awareness after finally surviving the many attempts of Saul to take his life. David has now defeated giants, overcome kings, and conquered tens of thousands of soldiers in battle. He knows what it means to be forced to accept life's changes in the midst of desiring rest and security.

> Then David spoke to the LORD the words of this song, on the day when the LORD had delivered him from the hand of all his enemies, and from the hand of Saul.
>
> And he said: "The LORD is my rock and my fortress and my deliverer;
> The God of my strength, in whom I will trust;
> My shield and the horn of my salvation,
> My stronghold and my refuge; My Savior, You save me from violence.
> I will call upon the LORD, who is worthy to be praised;
> So shall I be saved from my enemies."
>
> (2 SAMUEL 22:1–4)

May we reach this stage of maturity in our lives when we are no longer surprised by change. May we proclaim and sing like David that we know there's only one place to build where the storm can't destroy our house, only one place to stand where the wind can't sweep us into the storm. When we can reach this level of maturity, then our expectations become more realistic regarding the nature of change and its inevitability. This is the kind of maturity to which we aspire in facing the ups and downs in our workplace. The unexpected *will* happen, even as God remains sovereign and in control. He knows what will happen and how it fits His plan even when we can't see it.

NEXT-LEVEL LIVING

One way to mature in your handling of change is to remind yourself of your purpose and to view the transition as a means to your next level. Many of us want to go to that next level, to grasp the next rung on the ladder, to crash through the glass ceiling, but we aren't willing to stretch to get there. But truthfully, the only way we can extend ourselves to reach the next level is to move beyond our comfort zone and utilize more of our talents and capabilities. We must be willing to risk, move, take action. But even when we're sluggish, fearful, and resistant, God can still overcome our inertia and use us. When we don't move on our own, He introduces some change into our lives to spur us into action. The least we can do in turbulent times of change is to give Him the opportunity to use us, even when what we face seems formidable or impossible to us.

We see this in the transformation of Moses from a reluctant recluse to a dynamic director of God's purposes for His people. Appearing to Moses in the burning bush, God acknowledges the cries of His children in bondage and explains His plan for their release to Moses.

> "Come now, therefore, and I will send you to Pharaoh that you may bring My people, the children of Israel, out of Egypt."
>
> But Moses said to God, "Who *am* I that I should go to Pharaoh, and that I should bring the children of Israel out of Egypt?"
>
> (EXODUS 3:10–11)

God replies not by informing Moses who he is but by reinforcing who He is.

> "I will certainly be with you. And this shall be a sign to you that I have sent you. When you have brought the people out of Egypt, you shall serve God on this mountain."
>
> (EXODUS 3:12)

Moses goes on to pose the problems that he sees with God's plan, particularly the part involving Moses as His mouthpiece. "Who shall I say has sent me?" Moses asks, "What shall I tell them Your name is?" To which God responds, "Tell them I AM has sent me to you." (Exodus 3:13–14)

After the two exchange more details about God's plan, Moses comes up with another excuse:

> Then Moses said to the LORD, "O my Lord, I am not eloquent, neither before nor since You have spoken to Your servant; but I am slow of speech and slow of tongue."
>
> So the LORD said to him, "Who has made man's mouth? Or who makes the mute, the deaf, the seeing, or the blind? Have not I, the LORD?
>
> "Now therefore, go, and I will be with your mouth and teach you what you shall say."
>
> But he said, "O my Lord, please send by the hand of whomever else You may send."
>
> So the anger of the LORD was kindled against Moses, and He said: "Is not Aaron the Levite your brother? I know that he can speak well. And look, he is also coming out to meet you. When he sees you, he will be glad in his heart.
>
> "Now you shall speak to him and put the words in his mouth. And I will be with your mouth and with his mouth, and I will teach you what you shall do.
>
> "So he shall be your spokesman to the people. And he himself shall be as a mouth for you, and you shall be to him as God."
>
> (EXODUS 4:10–16)

Now in his mind, Moses probably thinks that this is his best excuse yet, and perhaps his concern is entirely legitimate

and sincere. Certainly it can be hard to see how to do the job
to which God is calling you if you don't have the prerequisites
for the position. How often have you told God why you
couldn't do something He asked you to do? "But, Lord, I'm terrified of talking in front of people, what do you mean you want
me to chair this meeting?" "Dear God, please don't ask me to
write this grant proposal—you know that my grammar skills
need serious help!" "Father, you know I don't have the computer skills needed for that position—why would you want me
to apply for something when I'm not qualified?"

Once again, this is where we cannot rely on our own perspective. We have to trust that God knows our strengths as
well as our limitations and yet He has still chosen us for the
job. In other words, He will provide everything we need, as we
need it, in order to fill the role and do the job. The only qual-
ification that we absolutely must have to do any job is an
anointing from the Lord. The rest, as they say, becomes "on-
the-job training." We simply have to trust Him and act on His
urging. If that means we tell Him our excuses and fears, then so
be it, as long as we're willing to act on faith.

This is not to say that you must never be afraid, insecure,
or flooded with feelings of inferiority. Like Moses, you may
feel so inadequate for the job you've been assigned that you
can't even imagine your success in this new role. This is when
you exercise your faith, stretching and growing beyond what
you can imagine, and simply do what needs doing based on
what you know.

This can be a humbling experience. You will likely find yourself more dependent on God than ever before, particularly if you feel underequipped for where He has called you to serve. You may have to ask a lot of questions to those around you, and sometimes more than once. Don't be afraid to ask, to make mistakes, to seek assistance from others, or to do things differently than your predecessor. *You are the man for the job! You are the woman for the job!* Don't lose sight of this truth in the midst of daunting obstacles and cataclysmic changes.

STAY IN CHARACTER

Like Moses's journey from the flocks he had been tending to the foyers of a royal palace, David also faced an abrupt change of locale. And with this scene switch, all the rules seem to have been changed. Where once David fought bears and lions preying on his sheep, suddenly he finds himself confronted with an evil-afflicted king bent on the young shepherd's destruction. Where once he had been out beneath the stars composing poetry in praise of his God, David finds himself in a standing-room-only concert for one as he played his harp to soothe the savage Saul. Where once he had been the youngest, most overlooked member of a large family, David finds himself anointed for the highest position in the land, with authority over every member of the nation.

Even in the midst of all these changes, David grasps the

fundamental truth of the situation quicker than Moses seems to have processed it. *He was the man for the job!* It's that simple. Time and time again, we must remember that when God anoints us for a position (our first commandment of working in a hostile environment), then nothing can ultimately stand in our way. In fact, if Moses is an example, we may be our own largest obstacle to getting the job done. Our perception of ourselves, if not based on faith in what we cannot presently see, will cause us to limit ourselves and undermine the blessing and success that God has planned for us. We are short-circuiting our own destiny, pulling the plug before the on switch has been flipped, all because we don't think we're adequately equipped for the job.

Once we realize that even if we can't see why God wants us in our present position we are still required to act, then we can begin to be ourselves. I've had several men and women come to me for counsel regarding a new job or new promotion that they have just received. While they know they are the right person for the job, they struggle to know how to act in their new role. As obvious as it may sound, I always ask them, "Other than God's will, what got you into that job?" In other words, what aspects of their character made their employer give them their new position? If being prompt, courteous, creative, and committed got you into the new role, then don't lose sight of these strengths by trying to fit into some preconceived mold.

It's tempting to believe that when we enter a new job or get promoted that we must change the way we act, the way we dress and speak. The personal assistant who advances into her boss's vacant position may think that she must act more like her boss—assertive, terse, intense, and focused—when in reality her own strengths that got her the job may be very different from her predecessor's. She may be gentle, calm, organized, and an excellent communicator. She doesn't need to pretend to be her boss or have his attributes.

You need to take your character with you when change occurs. In the theater, when an actor is onstage and forgets his or her next lines, they are trained to remain "in character." This simply means that even though they can't remember the exact lines of dialogue that their character should speak, the actor can quickly improvise based on who they know their character to be. Since most actors usually seek to understand the motives and desires of their roles, to know the essence of who their character truly is and how that character interacts with other characters, they can simply use this knowledge, along with the context of the spot where they forget their lines, to create a new script.

Similarly, you need to stay "in character" when change comes and you feel caught in the spotlight without knowing your lines. Don't put on airs of superiority, especially if you now oversee employees who were once your peers. While you may be required to update your wardrobe or change the name-plate on your door, don't try to play a role that doesn't reflect who you really are.

HOLDING PATTERN

Certainly not all of the changes you will face in your workplace involve your advancement. Sometimes they will involve being passed over for that promotion that you think you so richly deserve or receiving mixed signals from your supervisor regarding what your responsibilities are. And when you are laid off, fired, or feel led to quit by God's Spirit, then you face an entirely new spectrum of changes. Like a flight that had departed for Los Angeles only to discover an electrical storm near LAX, you may have to accept a holding pattern and wait to see what the next step will be. Or you may not be cleared for landing at the destination with which you began your journey; instead you are rerouted to a new runway.

These kinds of changes are often the most difficult and stressful to endure. You want to trust that God has something better for you, but when the bills need to be paid or you're feeling unwanted and of no value in a place that once esteemed your gifts, it can be extremely challenging. As much as you can, I encourage you not to take these kinds of events personally. During such tumultuous turnovers, you will need to focus on three key areas during the transition.

First, you must continue to take care of yoursel   ~v dimension of your life. The tendency is to feel dep frustrated, and down on yourself. You let you flounder to regain your balance from the fa' dazed and disoriented. Since you don't have to get up and go to the office, you decide that you might as well stay in your pajamas all day. Then the next day you don't shower or comb your hair, and the next you stay in bed, until a week has passed. No, I encourage you to follow your daily personal routines as much as possible during times of difficult transition. Wake at the usual time, shower, dress, eat breakfast, and make a list of objectives for that day. Maintain your best grooming and personal hygiene. Look to friends and family for emotional and spiritual support. Continue or even begin an exercise routine to help you cope with the stress. Do everything possible to take good care of your mind, body, heart, and soul during this time when change forces you into a new season. Look for opportunities to improve yourself during this interval.

The second area that requires your utmost attention is your career. You should take advantage of every resource offered by your previous employer. Many companies offer counseling, resume clinics, and computer access to employees who have been laid off or terminated. While you may be understandably angry and hurt by your employer's decision, you must not allow these feelings to prevent you from utilizing the employer's resources.

Networking offers another reason not to burn any bridges unless absolutely necessary—and sometimes it is. But to the extent that you can remain on cordial terms with former bosses, coworkers, or employees, you will likely find such relationships vital in your search for new employment opportunities.

Don't be afraid to ask for references when it's appropriate or even for names of other contacts.

As you focus on your career during this interval, consider taking a skills course at your local university, church, or library. Work at improving your area of expertise. Stay current on the latest developments in your field by reading the newest books and periodicals. Update your resume. Journal about your ultimate goals for your career. Look at what's holding you back and ask the Lord to remove those barriers according to His perfect will.

Which brings us to the third essential area for surviving and thriving during a critical change: prayer. While you were likely praying about your job prior to this transition time, you will want to saturate yourself in conversation with your Father in order to maintain your peace and in order to hear His voice for where He wants to take you next. As Paul instructed the Thessalonians: "Rejoice always, pray without ceasing, in everything give thanks; for this is the will of God in Christ Jesus for you" (I Thessalonians 5:16–18).

It can be particularly challenging to rejoice in the midst of losing your job or being unsure of where your next position will emerge. However, you must trust that your Father will provide for you and that He is preparing you for the next job. And don't be so proud that you can't ask others for help or accept it when they offer. God delights in using us to bless each other's lives—don't rob others of the blessing they receive by ministering to you in your need.

Ask others to pray for you and to give you wisdom in making decisions. This area can become particularly cloudy as you become tempted to take matters into your own hands and rely on your own abilities rather than waiting on God. Instead stay focused on His Word and keep the lines of communication open and clear between the two of you.

TONGUE-TIED

Communications between you and others in your workplace opens up another area where change often induces stress and strife. Whether it's conflict management, customer service, team building, or your annual performance review, good communication skills are essential. As problems and issues arise in the workplace—as they always do—you will be forced to become a translator, negotiator, diplomat, and peacekeeper. Nothing is more frustrating than being misunderstood, misheard, ignored, or misconstrued.

But sometimes talking isn't the answer. Often our problem is that we give too much verbiage to problems; in other words, we talk about them when we should actually be focusing on their solution. If peace is missing, don't talk about chaos; live at peace. God has given you the very gifts you will need to change the atmosphere of your work environment. Don't talk about it! Do it!

Talking can also take us further away from the solutions we

seek if we misuse words and talk out of hand. W
some expert and much-needed teaching in the Body of Christ
about our words and how we spend more time in regret than in
control of our tongue. James talks about the tongue and its im-
mense power for destruction: "Even so the tongue is a little
member and boasts great things. See how great a forest a little
fire kindles!" (James 3:5). To see this in action, you only have
to watch and observe how a conversation can start with just an
attitude in someone's voice pattern and then escalate into a
four-alarm fire!

Often in the workplace people are just waiting for some
brave, loose-tongued person to vent what they wished they
had the nerve to say and thus open the door so more fuel can
be thrown on the fire! Don't be that person with flames coming out of your mouth like some fire-eater in the circus! Learn
to stomp that flicker out before somebody blows air on it! If
you truly want to move from the rung of the ladder where you
are now and move higher to God, tame that tongue! Your
mouth can talk you out of more blessings than you can count.

We see this truth actualized once again by our boy David.
Notice his response to what was happening in the palace as he
arrives on the scene: a king afflicted by an evil spirit on his way
out of the palace even as his newly anointed successor arrives.
David wasn't stupid; he surely knew a whole lot about what was
going on—probably more than anybody there. But he didn't talk
about it. He kept it to himself. Remember the Psalm that says
"Pour out your complaint before God" (142:2). Not to cowork-

ers, employers, the janitor, the vendors who come into the work environment . . . no, only before God! Just tell Jesus! Unfortunately this seems so difficult for many Christians to grasp, particularly regarding the workplace. We should never be party to a bunch of disgruntled, complaining gripers! Grab ahold of that situation when it arises and bring light and life to it! Our conversations are to be seasoned with grace. Speak positively, because God is still on the throne and has a plan. A Christian has great power in the workplace with his tongue and with only a few words can change a whole lot of attitudes. At the very least, we can use the words we speak to draw a line in the sand and show a contrast to those who complain, gossip, backstab, and lie.

And then sometimes, it is just better to remain quiet. Don't be a party to needless conversation. "In quiet and confidence shall be your strength" (Isaiah 30:15). Thoughts are the final frontier of privacy. If we always speak our mind, we are violating our own privacy. When it is appropriate, speak up and speak right. But most of the time, we need to keep a guard on our lips. Refuse to reduce yourself to low levels of communication that serve as avenues for the devil to enter!

David *responded* to what was going on around him. That is different from reacting. Responding requires first quietness and then reflecting. Reacting suggests that some action takes place following a comment or an incident. We would be better off if we spent more time responding than we do reacting. Why don't we just spare them the piece of our mind and give them the peace our silence can offer?

ACTIONS SPEAK LOUDER

Along these lines, we don't have to talk about our faith for it to influence those around us on the job. The workplace is not the place for overt evangelism. Instead, we must behave as a follower of Jesus and let the difference speak for itself. Simply by the way we live out our Christian faith in the workplace we can become a catalyst for change.

You must remember your calling to be in this workplace at this time. Jesus came down to earth where things were a mess, and yet God had a specific reason for sending Him, the Prince of Peace, into the world of chaos. You, too, are on some assignment that can make a world of difference in someone's life . . . even the difference between their going to heaven or hell. That can be a fairly sobering thought. You may not be witnessing, but you can sure practice your prayer life and live like a living Bible, being a key witness.

And how do we keep our enthusiasm and passion for our faith fresh and energized? We should not be looking for this kind of boost from our workplace. No, we must fuel our faith from our home and our church home. God is so considerate in timing church services between workweeks. We ought to be in a church that builds us up so much on Sunday morning that we walk into that office on Monday morning with fresh fire for the enemy.

When you go to your place of employment these thoughts

should be running through your mind: "I'm the person for this job; thank You, Lord, for yet another opportunity to bring You into this place. Thank You, Lord, that when I walk in, the Spirit of the Lord has entered and I'm ready to enter the enemy's camp with all my weapons in place. That's okay, Sally; you don't need to smile at me. I'll just smile at you because Jesus is smiling at me. I hear Your voice, Lord. You're telling me that I can do all things through Christ who strengthens me. I see you glaring at me, Harold, but I'm happy in my soul 'cause Jesus died for me on the cross. I have a reason to be here and it's a Divine purpose. I refuse to get caught up in fruitless chatter and idle gossip. I will not fear the changes that this day may bring my way because God has gone before me."

This kind of prayerful self-talk can serve as a lifesaver when the hostility grows hotter. Feeding the mind on Truth will result in godly behavior, which eventually will radically change any environment. And while it is changing the environment, it is also radically and supernaturally changing you as you realize that even a part-time job requires full-time Christianity!

So don't fear change. Embrace every opportunity for change as a step closer to God's plan for your life. Accept every change in your workplace as allowed by God for His purposes!

FOURTH COMMANDMENT:

DO THE JOB WELL
WHILE REMEMBERING
THE VISION

S OMETIMES the greatest hostility in our workplace may actually come from inside of us. We look at our job compared to the jobs of others in the company or the positions of our friends and begin to feel envious. How often have you thought or even said, "I am so overqualified for this job! I can't believe that I'm even willing to take this kind of pay to do this kind of work. I'm so much better than this! I should be in that manager's office calling the shots. I should be in the boardroom making the decisions!" Assuming that there's truth in these statements, that you truly are overqualified for the position you hold, then doing your job well becomes a matter of exercising even more faith. And the secret to performing your duties well without becoming disgruntled or bored by your position is to maintain a vision of where you're headed in the future. Such a vision becomes the antidote for the toxic comparisons and covetousness of your present situation.

DOUBLE VISION

Contentment is a funny thing. It requires a balance between knowing you are in the place where God wants you in the present even as you anticipate and hope for the future for which He's preparing you. We have to keep one eye on our present position and give all that we can to perform our responsibilities with efficiency and professionalism. And at the same time, we must keep the other eye on the future position God has in store for us. We must assume that God has His reasons for training us for greater things by using our present environment. With this in mind, we must learn all that we can from our current situation. As I have stressed before, this includes both practical job skills, like how to run an Excel spreadsheet or plan a corporate event for five hundred people, as well as learning how to be more patient, to control your tongue, or to get along with diverse personalities. Both the skills and the character qualities will be needed to empower your next steps on the journey. Please don't overlook one at the expense of the other; both are part of why God has you where you are.

At the same time, we must not become resigned to always working in our current "dead-end" job even when we can't see what's behind the wall at the end of the alley. We should not feel locked in to the same level of our company or even to the same career field. We must not allow discouragement, or worse, despair, to impair our vision of our true capabilities and our ultimate destiny. He often requires that we wait patiently on His timing to move us into the position He has opened up for us. Don't forget that David was anointed as king at a very young age but wasn't *crowned* king until several years later. He was forced to wait even though the path for his destiny had already been cleared. David used the interval to become more mature, more reliant on God, and more politically aware of the position he was about to fill.

When you maintain this kind of double vision—making the most of your present position while anticipating the future God has planned for you—then you can see your way more clearly to trust Him as He guides and directs you.

Even without having that vision of where you're going, you should be committed to performing to the best of your ability in the workplace. Why? Perhaps the first and foremost reason stems from your desire to be a good steward of these responsibilities with which God has charged you. You should want to please Him first before you please yourself and those for whom you labor. Whether you are presently busing tables or busing children to school, you should perform your tasks as if you are literally doing it for your King. Those are His dirty dishes that you are clearing from that crumb-strewn counter. Those are His children that you have been entrusted to transport from home to school and back again. Working first to serve your Heavenly Father deflates any attempts by your ego to compare and denounce your present position. Instead of feeling like you're wasting time, you begin to realize that what you're doing counts for eternity. As crazy as it may seem, He wants to use you in His purposes even when you're ringing up groceries, painting houses, selling cars, balancing books, or adjusting claims.

Such a perspective creates a wonderfully focused picture of who you are in Christ. Any hostilities in your environment that would mar the picture become minor specks to be dusted away. Just as people have two eyes but one field of vision (instead of seeing two of everything!), when we make God's purpose our centerpiece, then our double vision of our present job and future goal will converge into one beautiful scene.

WITNESS STAND

In a courtroom trial, witnesses are frequently called by both sides to testify to what they saw and experienced at the scene of the crime. These people are active participants in the legal process as much as the attorneys, defendant, judge, and jury. And any good prosecutor will tell you that it's often not so much what the witness on the stand actually says as much as his body language and the way he says it. Everything from the witness's appearance and grooming to his speech patterns and mannerisms testify to those observing him.

Similarly you testify as a witness on your job every working day. Controlling your tongue and being an effective communicator are both important, as we've seen. But the greatest testimony to your Christian faith rises from your actions, interactions, and satisfactions. Your behavior individually, your encounters with others, and your level of contentment all sing out loud and clear about what you truly believe.

When you perform your job well, it's clear that you adhere to a standard of excellence. And your witness will be noticed. You do not have to tell anyone yourself; your actions will scream at them to take notice of who you are and what you're about. This will reflect on you and your gifts and talents certainly. But if you carry out your job in a spirit of humility and give others credit where due and acknowledge God as the ultimate Source of your abilities, then you become a living testimony to Christ in a way that others can't dismiss.

If you weighed the impact that a preacher, pastor, or even an evangelist has on the world, it could not compare to the potential a Christian in the world is afforded. We need to operate in our workplace with such high standards because the world is watching. Ideally, people should be coming to the Church for everything from help in raising their children to making world decisions. However, before this can ever come to fruition, Christians need to present a good, solid case to the world that we do, in fact, have the Truth-filled solutions they need.

There is nothing wrong with door-to-door witnessing or any form of evangelism that leads people to Jesus, but out in the workplace, sinners need to see some examples of high-quality workmanship. They need to see us not only getting the job done, but performing at a standard of excellence. They don't need to hear us preaching, nor do we need to be leading prayer groups in the cafeteria. Quite the contrary, for I fear that sometimes we, as believers, unintentionally permit our faith to undermine our work performance. Whether it's using company time to try and build a discipling relationship or to steer a conversation toward Christ, or making copies of the flier for your church's revival on the office copier, this is not the impression you want to create.

I recall a situation where a director of a preschool had employed a very gifted young teacher. She was creative and talented. Her interaction with the students created a positive learning environment where these underprivileged children gained self-esteem and confidence. But this young teacher had just become a Christian and had a real sincere zeal for serving the Lord, so she spent time each morning before work "witnessing" to people in her neighborhood. The problem was, she was chronically late for work. The witness that she needed to provide was getting to work on time so that the other workers were not inconvenienced by the unsupervised children that her tardiness afforded. The problem was resolved after the director spoke with her, but the witness had already been impaired. We need to understand that people really don't want to hear about Jesus as much as they want to see the benefits of Christianity at work in someone's life on a continuous basis.

So which benefits will impress an employer most? While there are numerous individual benefits that may vary from person to person, virtually all employers will be impressed with punctuality, reliability, and dependability. Regardless of your level of abilities, these three are all within the realm of your control. If you demonstrate these qualities in your workplace, your actions will shout your faith louder than if you brought in a street preacher during coffee break. You see, the work ethic in this country has eroded and management is crying out for people who will show up for work, do their job responsibly, and not steal from the company. It sounds so simple, but reliable people with positive attitudes and a professional demeanor are difficult to come by and to keep. A friend who recruits for a large company once told me that "a good man is hard to find and a good woman is hard to keep!"

Thankfully, it's not up to us to be perfect employees. We simply need to rely on Him. God espouses our efforts to be living examples of ethics in the workplace. But we *are* required to make an effort. The impression we create as Christians can carry over into all aspects of how we perform our job. Even the appearance of a person's desk can emit a message about the person's work habits. It certainly doesn't have to be spotless, but some sense of order and organization go a long way in creating a positive impression. Consider the message that's transmitted if our coworkers consistently see us buried beneath files that should have been filed, messages that should have been responded to, and there on a stack of coffee-stained documents sits our desk rock: "I can do all things through Christ who strengthens me." They may be thinking, "All things? He can't even help you keep your desk straight!"

SHOW ME THE MISSION

We want our witness to be positive, and it will likely have more power if it's covert and subtle rather than zealous and verbal. If we walk through the Bible to learn patterns of how God operates, we will discover that He has always been in the business of sending out spies and warriors. Our battles are of a different nature than those His followers in ancient times faced, but they involve warfare nonetheless. And our warfare demands different approaches today. We dress up in a suit and go to work where devils dress up in suits as well. We don't even have different uniforms. So if God wants to subdue some enemies, perhaps some corruption to be exposed, He will select a good, faithful Christian who understands "undercover work."

In our modern world, God sees the injustice, prejudice, racism, fraud, embezzlement, and all the forms of harassment that exist and grow like cancer where innocent people work every day trying to earn a decent living. Doesn't it seem likely that a compassionate God who is "kind to all the works of His hands" would wince at all that injustice and feel compelled to intervene? So you, Christian, are on a mission.

There is no other motivator that can sustain you. It's not about the money; God could send checks in the mail, arrange inheritances, endowments, or just stuff a few hundred-dollar bills in the laundry detergent box. However, I'm afraid that without a monetary reward system in place, there would be few people who would ever go to work. There is nothing wrong with money and everybody needs it, but receiving revenue should not be the Christian's primary reason for work.

For the Christian, a job is a place where God can get His work accomplished and pay His children to do it. If He wants them on the job full-time after they have been faithful part-time, God will arrange favor to surround them so that their boss "somehow" becomes aware of their faithfulness, maturity, promptness, and diligence. He will highlight their gifts and arrange divine appointments with the right people at the right time. Say it every morning while you're brushing your hair: "Lord, I thank You for favor and for ordering my steps today!" God is simply paying a child of His to be the salt and light in a hostile environment while He trains His child to be prepared for Divine destiny. What a deal!

It deserves repeating: The primary reason for employment should not be the revenue. Instead of "show me the money," it should be show me the mission!

I am not at all suggesting that you not get paid for your

work. The hireling is worthy. What I am saying is that the attitude of your heart should always be service to God. He is
the Source anyhow, anyway! If you allow yourself to be
guided by money, it will only serve to undermine the mission.
Remember, money is not the mission! Some places may hardly pay
you at all what you're worth, but your value is with God and
He is in control. If you make money your god, it will control
all your decisions. You need to be careful that you don't pros-
titute yourself to the highest bidder, miss the mission, and
forfeit God's purpose. Money, my friend, is to fund the mission!

The vision God has given you is not going to be funded by
one stream. God gave Adam four streams of provision. You're
not different; God is no respecter of persons. Long before your
little feet hit this planet, God had placed dreams, visions, gifts,
and talents deep within you. All of that came from Him, so
surely He will enable you to put them to work just where He
would like them to manifest. A Christian in today's society
should have many "streams of revenue" available. The job
should never be our only financial river, but one of several.

Some of you might just be realizing that there's another gift
surfacing in your life. Embrace it, polish it, pray over it, sur-
render it, and watch God make it flourish! Don't let people
label and compartmentalize you; you are not *just* a teacher, for
instance. You may teach, but you may also have a remarkably
strong gift of money management and be able to counsel those
who struggle with budgeting and investment. You may be a

factory worker but also handy enough to build furniture. So you create a side business. There is so much you can do, so make your talents work for you.

It is never too late to say to God, "Lord, I know there's more. I've worked for the almighty dollar all my life, but I am so unfulfilled. Reach down inside me, Lord, and bring up that deposit. I want to be available for You, so surface those gifts. Thank You for showing me, Lord, that money is an enablement, not an attainment. Help me to stretch beyond myself and all my needs and to care about the concerns on Your heart. Help me to be motivated, passionate, and ignited by the dreams You have predetermined for my brief interlude on earth. I am trusting You, Lord, to dredge up those streams of generous and endless supply that You have entrusted to me that I might be a blessing to someone else. Thank You, Lord, for removing deception and raining down Truth so that I can truly see that I am here to bring You glory! In no other name but Jesus, Amen!"

VISION QUEST

Even in the midst of doing your job well and being a magnetic witness for the faith, you must cultivate a vision for where you are going. Scripture tells us that people perish without a vision (Proverbs 29:18). You must be in pursuit of the hopes and dreams that God has planted in you and are growing in you even as you water and nourish that seed in the soil of your present position.

Sometimes it's easy to cultivate that vision and imagine your natural progression from your present employment all the way to the top of the industry. You were fortunate to discover your calling at an early age and perhaps even more blessed to find someone to pay you for your passion. Maybe you entered your field right out of college, working in the office doing clerical work, but your eye for business and your shrewd instincts serve as a natural bridge for you to rise in the company. Therefore it's easy to imagine yourself as president of the company or as an entrepreneur starting your own business.

Other times it may be challenging to know the direction that you should be heading in. You know you're in the place God wants you for the present, but you also know that it's not your life's work. Or your present situation may seem so very far from where you would like to be and believe God is calling you. You can't imagine getting from point A to point B because the two are just so different and far apart. But just because you can't connect your present position to your goals doesn't mean that you shouldn't cultivate those dreams.

Dreams are a vital part of everyone's vision. In fact, one of the best examples from Scripture relies on the meaning of dreams and a key person's ability to interpret the dreams of others. Like the young David being anointed long before he would actually become king, Joseph started out with bold dreams—where he was literally the center of the universe!

Now Joseph had a dream, and he told it to his brothers; and they hated him even more.

So he said to them, "Please hear this dream which I have dreamed:

"There we were, binding sheaves in the field. Then behold, my sheaf arose and also stood upright; and indeed your sheaves stood all around and bowed down to my sheaf."

And his brothers said to him, "Shall you indeed reign over us? Or shall you indeed have dominion over us?" So they hated him even more for his dreams and for his words.

Then he dreamed still another dream and told it to his brothers, and said, "Look, I have dreamed another dream. And this time, the sun, the moon, and the eleven stars bowed down to me."

So he told it to his father and his brothers; and his father rebuked him and said to him, "What is this dream that you have dreamed? Shall your mother and I and your brothers indeed come to bow down to the earth before you?"

And his brothers envied him, but his father kept the matter in mind.

(GENESIS 37:5–11)

Naturally, Joseph's siblings didn't like the idea of serving underneath their kid brother, so they decided to take matters into their own hands to prevent such a humiliating power play from ever happening. They faked his death and sold him into slavery to foreigners traveling abroad.

Now at this point Joseph was most likely feeling betrayed by his brothers. But I wonder if he was also feeling mocked by his own dream. How in the world would he ever rise to be a leader of his people from the shackles of slavery in Egypt? Perhaps you have felt this way when a chance you took toward reaching your dreams suddenly boomeranged back and hit you upside the head. You made an investment that you hoped would lead to the freedom to quit your present job and pursue your vision, only the investment failed and you lost your money. Or you took on that big project hoping to impress your boss and get the promotion you've been petitioning for, but the project fell apart and it looked like it was all your fault. You took steps to move toward your dream, but now it seems that you're worse off than when you started.

But even when the situation looks dire, God can turn things around. Joseph's predicament might have looked hopeless when he was sold, but from slavery he rose to household manager for Potiphar. "The Lord was with Joseph, and he was a successful man; and he was in the house of his master the Egyptian. So Joseph found favor in his sight, and served him" (Genesis 39:2–3). After all, Joeseph was gifted at managing resources and his work spoke for itself. God blessed him and used him according to the gifts that He had planted in him.

However, Joseph's story illustrates that life can be a roller coaster with many ups and downs. Just as his star is rising, Joseph becomes prey to Potiphar's wife and her own selfish desires. "Come lie with me," she tells him seductively. Joseph resists the married woman's advances, knowing that he will likely lose his job. But that is not the primary reason for resisting the advances of his master's wife. "How then can I do this great wickedness, and sin against God?" Because he is serving God first, Joseph knows that if he fails he will be disappointing God, and that's what's most important to him.

There's no indication that Joseph ever wavered in his convictions about resisting the adulterous advances of his boss's wife. But as smart as he was, he had to have realized that if he were to sleep with her, she could likely help him advance. Not only could he enjoy the sensual pleasure of sex, but he could actually further his career in the process. If he had done it, Joseph would not have been the first or the last to "sleep his way to the top" in his profession. But he did not want to sin against God, despite whatever negative consequences might occur. And negative consequences did come. Potiphar's wife hates Joseph's rejection so much that she frames him for raping her, ensuring that he not only will lose his job but will be jailed.

Have you ever experienced this kind of situation where you would likely be penalized for doing the right thing? Whether it's the temptation to succumb to the boss's advances in order to get your promotion or the decision to stand strong against the office bandwagon by not lying to your customers in order to make a sale, most of us face these situations every day. Like Joseph, we must keep our priorities straight and remember our primary purpose in life is to do God's will and live up to His expectations of us.

Now things really must have looked bleak for Joseph. From inside his prison cell, it must have been incredibly difficult to maintain the vision, to keep the faith, to believe that God had something extraordinary in store for him. It would have been so much easier to have a pity party, complain about life's injustice, and play the victim. But he did not fall for the enemy's attempts to derail him from his true destiny. As promised, God directs Joseph's path all along to bring him to a position of power and authority. In jail, Joseph encountered the butler and the baker for the Pharaoh, both men troubled by dreams that Joseph was able to accurately interpret for them. Eventually, Pharaoh himself experiences disturbing dreams that he can't interpret. Although we're told that two full years passed, the butler finally remembers his old cell buddy, Joseph. With his God-given ability to interpret the Pharaoh's dream, and the leader's subsequent impression of Joseph's ability and character, Joseph finds himself one of the most powerful men in the world. Quickly Pharaoh places him second in command, empowering Joseph to develop and execute a master plan for utilizing resources and surviving the impending famine.

And you likely know the rest of the story—when the famine comes and spreads to Joseph's homeland, his brothers travel to Egypt seeking food. Joseph is able to forgive his family because he has witnessed the hand of God operating in his life even when it felt like he had been abandoned. Even though his brothers and Potiphar's wife intended evil for Joseph, God turned it inside out and proceeded to lead Joseph to his destiny. "As for you, you meant evil against me; but God meant it for God" (Genesis 50:20). Countless lives were saved as God redeemed Joseph's losses and transformed them into stepping-stones to carry out His master plan.

And He does the same for us. No matter where you are right now, whether in a prison cell like Joseph or a soup kitchen in the inner city or at home with small children, God has not abandoned you of the dreams that He's seeded in your heart. You may not be able to imagine how to get from your present starting point to where your dreams would take you, but that's all right. Simply ask Him to reveal your next step, and then the next. Pray that He would increase the clarity and desire for your dreams. The more you can imagine yourself leading in the boardroom, launching your own business, writing your first novel, starring in your own play, or coaching others with your unique gifts, the sooner it will become reality. I'm convinced that God gives us glimpses first until our vision becomes clearer and stronger, like a picture developing from a soft blur into sharp resolution.

Take that vision and run with it. Allow it to fuel your motivation to perform to the best of your ability in your present position. And remain in constant communication with He who knows and loves you best. As you work at performing your present job well while cultivating and remembering your vision, you may find the following prayer helpful:

"Lord, I thank You for all that You have given me—even those things that seem unfair and unjust, even those scars that have been inflicted by those intending evil against me. Please strengthen my commitment to serve You first in all that I do. Allow me to do my best and to remain positive and hopeful because I know that this present job is not my ultimate destination. Grant me glimpses of Your vision for my future so that my hope might grow in accordance with Your timing. Give me patience along the way and faith to trust that You are working for my good every second of this very day. With thanksgiving in the name of Jesus, Amen."

DON'T LET
THE ENVIRONMENT GET
INSIDE OF YOU!

THE room is locked and sealed. Signs posted outside indicate an imminent danger for those who enter without protection. Only nurses and doctors visit the patient inside the room, always making sure that they are completely covered in proper attire to prevent the toxin from invading their bodies. Visitors are not allowed. Bold letters proclaim "Quarantine." Some disease, virus, or bacteria that can invade our bodies is suddenly loosed, potentially posing a health risk if other people are exposed to it. The sick person is forced into isolation until their condition changes and they are no longer contagious.

While this scenario happens in the medical field, a similar toxicity can invade the workplace. But it is not a virus or some parasite that threatens the workers that come in contact with it. No, it is something potentially more dangerous. Negative attitudes, harmful behavior, and insidious gossip can contaminate the believer and cause her to lose her witness, along with her peace, hope, and joy. When the hostile environment of the workplace gets inside of the believer, then she becomes isolated as well. While she may feel like she belongs and fits in with her coworkers, she becomes separated from her true purpose for being there. She loses her vision. She becomes vulnerable to other hostilities in the workplace until she gives up or else resigns herself to never going forward.

DIVINE DIET

My brothers and sisters, you must take a spiritual vaccine if you don't want to be contaminated by the hostile environment in which you work. There is no single shot that can protect you from the toxins in your workplace, but there are precautions you must take in order to protect yourself. The single most effective measure you can take is to attend to proper spiritual nutrition. When the pressures and hostilities build in your workplace, then having Truth inside you becomes all the more imperative. You must maintain a regular diet of prayer and Bible study. Focus on His Truth and feed on His Word. Make sure that you have the proper nourishment you need in order for your soul to thrive. Just as our bodies can become more susceptible to illness when we do not eat healthy foods, so can our minds and hearts. The old saying about "junk in, junk out" holds true. We must nourish our souls as well as our bodies if we are to remain strong. "Man shall not live by bread alone; but man lives by every word that proceeds from the mouth of the Lord" (Deuteronomy 8:3).

Once you feel confident in pursuing a regular diet of Divine sustenance, then you must look at other ways you can prevent the absorption of your work environment. And like any good doctor assessing his patient's well-being, you must identify the particular elements in your environment from which you need protection. What are the toxins of your particular workplace? Sometimes they are obvious—things like complainers, gripers, gossipers, backbiters, and harassers. When these agents come your way, you must quickly find something else that needs doing. Even if you have to go to the restroom, check messages on your cell, or refill your coffee cup to get away, I encourage you to have a plan when the office pollutants drift your way. Like secondhand smoke invading your lungs, just being around these toxins is dangerous and you must be prepared to remove yourself from the situation if necessary.

VACATE THE PREMISES

Other "germs" that you should not allow inside you are not as overt or as easy to avoid. Foremost among these is workaholism. Whether it is the expectation from your boss that trickles down to all employees or a self-induced state, workaholism compels you to do whatever it takes to complete the next project, update the next report, or prepare for the next big meeting. In short, your life is not your own. When this bug hits you, suddenly you don't have a life outside of the workplace, but strangely enough you may not have time to realize it because you're too busy! You're coming in early, skipping lunch as needed, staying late, taking work home, getting up and doing it all again.

Now please don't hear me wrong on this. Certainly we should be willing to go above and beyond when special circumstances dictate the need. This can be part of your witness as you make some personal sacrifices in order to get a particular job done. We should also make it a habit to give more than is required as much as possible. But what I'm talking about is chronic chaos mode, where there's always the "next big thing" demanding your time, attention, and energy. This becomes the typical routine, not the exception. Everyone in the office accepts this unspoken policy and it becomes socially acceptable, despite the fact that the entire office staff has become a group of exhausted adrenaline junkies. When this is the atmosphere of your workplace, then you will quickly burn out and angrily resent all those who pressured you into overextending yourself. Most of all, you will resent yourself for being used in this way.

With a few possible exceptions, my advice is to maintain your boundaries between your work life and the rest of your life. When it's time to leave, don't linger just to impress someone else. Vacate the premises. Learn to separate business from pleasure. Even if you work with friends or become friends with some of your coworkers, make every effort to maintain firm boundaries between your professional and social lives. Try to discuss work matters only at work, not at church, over dinner, or during the racquetball game. Similarly, keep the personal matters out of the boardroom. Work is work and shouldn't be about social discussions of this season's hottest fashions or a play-by-play recap of last night's ballgame.

Work is also not the place to air your personal problems and ask for advice and counsel. Your coworkers are not there to unknot your issues or to make you feel good. And even if they enjoy playing the role of therapist, this type of relationship at work draws both of you away from the work at hand. You must also realize that placing someone in this position can negatively affect the way they view your job performance. You may not be asked to tackle the next big assignment because your team leader assumes you're still preoccupied with the marital problems you shared with her last week. If you are so upset or emotionally distraught over a personal matter, then take a personal day if possible and talk it out with a close friend, mentor, counselor, or pastor. And don't forget to pray!

Work is also not a dating service. When you're scoping out the hottie in human resources or the cutie in accounting, it's hard to focus on your job. A major preoccupation develops that drains energy away from your responsibilities and your witness. Perhaps you have experienced a relationship with a coworker that you found bright, attractive, and available. He or she may have even been a believer. However, I strongly encourage you to refrain from dating a coworker. Perhaps some couples met on the job and this led to a serious relationship and then to marriage, but in the majority of instances, couples who work together and date each other face consequential problems. Most of these relationships don't work out and this in turn creates a new tension in the workplace between the two of you. Even if you've agreed to "remain friends" and keep your work roles professional, the underlying awkwardness lingers on like the smell of spoiled food long after the refrigerator has been cleaned out. Couples in this situation also believe that no one else in the office knows about their romance or about the breakup that followed. However, the truth of the matter is that these types of things rarely go unnoticed by those around you. Whether it's the look in your eyes, the tone of your speech, or your body language around each other, your coworkers will notice. They may even make assumptions about the nature of your relationship no matter how pure you may be working to keep it. Your office mates will definitely view you differently when you're dating someone from the workplace.

Clearly here I'm addressing those of you who are single. It goes without saying that those of you who are married must refrain from making or taking any improper advances to or from someone in your workplace. Even if you consider it "harmless" flirtation, others will make assumptions about your character that bruise your professional reputation as well as your spiritual testimony. Make an effort to remain beyond reproach in your dealings with coworkers. Whether married or single, you should show respect, courtesy, and kindness to other people—these are the best ways to prevent the danger of lust or emotional entanglement from taking root inside you.

PLAY OUTSIDE

Another way to inoculate yourself from the germs of hostility in your work environment is to have outside interests. You need to play outside the office. Make sure you recharge and rejuvenate yourself with hobbies and pursuits away from the workplace and your field of business. It's tempting to think we don't have time for personal endeavors such as drawing, making jewelry, playing softball, baking, swimming, or reading the latest novel, but I'm here to tell you that if you don't allow yourself these pleasures, then you are going to burn out. You must reward yourself for the labor that you expend at your workplace.

Finding a sport, activity, or form of exercise that you enjoy is an excellent way to beat the stress generated by your job. Physical activity builds both your body's immune system as well as your mind's. Whether it's a spinning class, aerobics, ballroom dancing, intramural basketball, weight training, kayaking, or Rollerblading, once you find a physical activity that you enjoy (or at least can tolerate!), then it serves as a release valve for the elements of your hostile work environment that may have built up inside you.

Meeting new people and cultivating relationships that are totally unrelated to work is another good way to give yourself a mental vacation. We all need a place where we don't have to be the secretary, the team member, the boss, the computer fixer, copy machine coaxer, or coffee fetcher. Instead, we can relate as peers, as friends, like David did when he met Saul's son Jonathan. The two of them formed such a strong, intense bond that served as a safe place for both of them. As Saul's hatred for David escalated, Jonathan literally saved his friend's life. Christian friends who know us outside of our roles in the workplace can give us soul nourishment that we can never receive from our coworkers.

REMEMBER THE SABBATH

Perhaps the greatest way to ensure your proper health, on all levels, is the way that God Himself ordained.

And on the seventh day God ended His work which He had done, and He rested on the seventh day from all His work which He had done. Then God blessed the seventh day and sanctified it, because in it He rested from all His work which God had created and made.

(GENESIS 2:2–3)

Having sanctified this day of rest for Himself, it's not surprising that He passes it along to His children. "Remember the Sabbath day, to keep it holy" (Exodus 20:8). While God didn't need the physical rest the way our bodies do, He certainly appreciates the need for mental and spiritual rest. As we are created in His image, in frail mortal bodies, how much more do we need to attend to the Sabbath?

We might wonder how much Saul abided by this commandment. While we're not told that he didn't keep the Sabbath, in my thinking there is a correlation between spiritual unrest and affliction and not attending to the weariness of our bodies and souls. It's David's harp playing, the soothing sounds of music, that offer solace and comfort for the agitated, evil afflicted king. I'm convinced that if we don't make room for the Sabbath in our lives on a regular basis, then we are setting ourselves up for physical illness, mental fatigue, and emotional burnout.

Originally, the Sabbath was the seventh day of the week, now our Saturday, when the Jews deliberately set aside their work, including most household chores and personal tasks, in order to rest and focus on God. They prepared food ahead of time, let cleaning and cooking wait, set aside the urgent, and practiced being still before their Lord. The day was spent in worship, in quiet, prayerful reflection, in tranquility before the next cycle of busyness began with the new week.

Foremost, you need this time spiritually to equip yourself for returning to the warfare of your workplace. The Sabbath should be like a soldier's furlough time when he returns home from the battlefront and gets some much-needed rest before he returns reequipped to confront the enemy. David knew this most essential practice well, as we see demonstrated in so many of his beautiful Psalms. He reminds us that the Lord wants us to "be still and know that I am God."

While we need to be spending time in prayer and the Word each day if possible, we also need a special time set aside to give our utmost attention to He who made us and created us for His purposes. When we quiet ourselves from the all the busy thoughts pinballing through our minds, we can restore our peace and hear His voice. In this holy time we discover more of His loving kindness toward us, more of His desire for us to discover the destiny that He has seeded in us. We are able to praise and worship Him in the intimacy of our heart's chapel. This is so instrumental to your overall well-being that I can't emphasize enough how much you must make room for this time of soul rest in your life.

Group worship and teaching that equips you in your faith should be key elements in your Sabbath. This is why having a good church home is so vitally important to any believer, but particularly those working in a hostile work environment. Because you face the battle daily, you need the extra nutrients and spiritual vitamins that Spirit-breathed teaching infuses into your system. This is certainly my goal and desire in sharing with you what God has so powerfully laid on my heart with these commandments.

R & R

In our country today I'm afraid we have lost the cultural sense of what it means to take a Sabbath. Instead of "rest and relaxation," R & R now might as well stand for "race and rampage." For our grandparents and even some of our parents, Sunday was usually a hallowed day of rest, recreation, and family times regardless of whether you were Christian or not. It wasn't unusual to sleep in late, read the Sunday paper in bed, get ready to go to church, have a big family lunch afterward, take a nap, play some board games or a neighborhood pickup game of basketball. Everyone seemed to set their cares aside and focus on their priorities of self-care, family time, and fun for its own sake.

However, in our twenty-first century breakneck-speed-nanosecond-overnight-delivery culture, Sunday is just another workday for many folks. Even if you don't have to punch your time clock or go into the office on that day, many people continue their hectic schedules on the weekend. We need to catch up on our laundry, pay the bills, go grocery shopping, get haircuts, buy clothes for the kids, attend soccer games, pick up the dry cleaning, wash the car, mow the grass, clean out the garage, make cookies for the church bake sale, and on and on it goes. Even going to the park with your kids or hosting a family dinner now becomes just another item to be checked off your to-do list. Events that were once leisurely and pleasurable have sadly become just more performance-pressure-inducing chores.

I understand these pressures of our modern lifestyle. And I appreciate and utilize many of the conveniences that they afford—cell phones, the Internet, e-mail, computers, and so forth. However, if we are to survive the hostile work environments into which we are called, if we are to see our faith grow and not erode by sheer exhaustion, then we must reclaim the Sabbath as a fundamental necessity.

While there are a variety of ways to practice your Sabbath, I suggest that you at least focus on the three areas I mentioned earlier: self-care, family time, and the pursuit of fun. Each one restores and replenishes the vital elements that your workplace depletes. Let's quickly consider each of these.

Taking good care of yourself is essential—not a luxury, mind you, but absolutely essential if you are to continue working successfully in your hostile environment. You should work hard and reward yourself with some pampering and personal pleasures. Whether it's a spa day, a massage or pedicure, a special bath time with candles and oils, buying yourself some beautiful flowers, taking a nap, making love with your spouse, or reading poetry or motivational writers, you must honor yourself. And I'm not just talking to the ladies here! Men, it's okay to admit that you enjoy a manicure or time in the sauna! When Jesus told us to love others as we love ourselves, He assumed that we know how to love ourselves. Too often when we get caught up in making a living, pursuing our career, and fulfilling our responsibilities, we lose sight of loving ourselves in healthy ways. And when we don't take regular care of ourselves in healthy ways, then we will either keep going until we crash—our bodies give out, our minds can't take it, or our hearts can't cope—or we will turn to illegitimate ways of making ourselves feel better—alcohol, drugs, over-spending, illicit sex, overeating.

Quality family time is also vital if you are to survive and thrive in your hostile work environment. For too long our families have suffered for the price of our employment. We tell our spouses and our children that we are working so hard so that they can enjoy the benefits. But at what point are we losing touch with those we love the most so that we can buy them the latest PlayStation or designer dress? While most of us say that our family comes first, we must act on this consistently if we want to prevent the contagious hostilities of our workplace from infecting us.

This means that you do your very best to attend those ball-games, piano recitals, school plays, and spelling bees. It means that you don't disconnect from your spouse in order to finish that report by Monday. It means that you set aside time each day and each week to come together as a family and support and nurture one another. While interacting with our families can be draining at times, we mustn't lose sight of the way that they also inspire, motivate, and encourage us with their love and faith. As hard as it may be, I encourage you to plan family outings, maintain family traditions, and set aside some time for nothing but family silliness and fun.

Which brings me to the third area that should be part of your Sabbath: the pursuit of fun. As adults most of us take ourselves far too seriously. We dress up in our business suits and speak in our carefully modulated voices and prepare somber reports written in the dry jargon of our industry. We avoid missing deadlines as if the world will end if we're late or make a mistake or need to ask someone else for assistance. We get caught in the trap of only focusing on the next acquisition, customer order, completed contract, or promotional achievement.

If we maintain this kind of professional intensity all of the time, we will become rigid, legalistic, and brittle. We lose our sense of humor, our willingness to ask for forgiveness, and our ability to extend grace to others. One of the best ways of keeping perspective on what's truly important—not just urgent—is to make sure that we leave room for fun in our lives.

As part of our Sabbath, we should allow for activities that bring us pleasure and fulfillment, whether it be playing cards with friends, playing sports with others in our community, or playing Monopoly with our children. Reading a good story or

watching an entertaining movie, attending a concert by our favorite artist, or watching our favorite team play can take us out
of ourselves. Play helps to restore our creativity, to fuel our
imaginations, and to restore balance in our work-lopsided
world. The tendency is that this is usually one of the most neg-
lected areas of our lives. We think we don't have time for fun.
But the truth is that we won't have enough time without it. No
one on her deathbed wishes for more time to file reports,
empty in-boxes, grade papers, or attend board meetings. But
many of us do wish we had more time to eat ice cream cones,
stroll in the park, listen to a beautiful aria, or tickle our kids on
the living room floor.

One place where all three of these areas—self, family, and
fun—converge is vacation. My observation is that for most of
us vacation has become more of a chore than a time of R & R.
We have to get ahead at work so that we can be gone for a
week, then we have to make all the preparations to travel, then
we have to try and let go of worrying about things at work
even as we try and ensure that the kids and everyone else is
having a good time. Then it's time to come home, unpack, and
gear up for Monday morning, where we'll face hundreds of e-
mails, phone messages, and forms piled up on our desk. It's no
wonder that we need a vacation from our vacation!

I recommend that you plan several vacations or mini-
vacations, such as a long weekend, and focus on one of these
three areas as the priority. While this may sound overly indul-
gent, I believe that it's the only way to truly get some rest, get

to know your family better, and get to have some fun. These vacations need not be expensive or incredibly exotic. Take a self vacation where you go somewhere by yourself and allow your instincts to dictate your schedule. Sleep as late as you can, eat when you're hungry, browse along an unfamiliar street. It can be very rejuvenating to be in a place where no one knows who you are, cares what you're doing, or wants something from you.

Similarly, plan a vacation where family unity is the priority, such as attending a family reunion, returning to the area where you or your spouse grew up, visiting grandparents or other relatives, or creating new traditions for holidays. I know one family that enjoys going on a cruise each year for Christmas—they love the time together in the exotic settings far more than the hustle and bustle of the traditional family activities and obligations during the holiday season.

And sometimes it's nice to plan a little getaway where having fun is the focus—taking a spontaneous road trip over a long weekend, a day's outing at the local amusement park, surprising your spouse with tickets to a play, even an afternoon at the beach or in the mountains. No agenda other than just cutting loose and having a little fun.

If you make practicing the Sabbath a reality, both spiritually as well as in the other dimensions of your life, you will be amazed at its impact on your attitude in the workplace. Take time to rest and then give your best!

CAPITAL GAINS

Another potential toxin in your workplace seeps through the veins of many businesses. In fact, it's arguably the lifeblood of our capitalist economic system. Ambition, avarice, and greed are often viewed positively by employers as they seek to undermine their competition and acquire their customers' hard-earned dollars. We're encouraged to work for higher salaries, monetary bonuses, and cash prizes. For many of us, our employers are motivated by profit margins and they assume that everyone else should be too. In the worst of situations, the love of money becomes their god and they worship it with a devotion that would put some of us believers to shame. When we embrace their false god, we lose our mission and sense of purpose, until one day we wake up and discover that their capital gains have become our spiritual losses.

The love of money usually works hand in glove with the pursuit of material possessions and accumulated wealth. The more money we make, the more our purchase power increases. Consumerism is an epidemic in our society that we must attempt to resist. We must stay focused on the truth that God provides abundantly for our needs and will take care of us beyond what we ourselves can imagine. His manna may not be in the form that we desire, but this is when we must trust His judgment to know what is best for us.

It's not easy to resist the pull of greed and material goods.

T. D. JAKES

When it's difficult to make ends meet, when we know we're being underpaid, even when we have what we need but not what we want, it can be hard to not become resentful of those who have more. Seeds of avarice give root to resentment and soon ugly fruits of bitterness bloom inside you. You find yourself tempted to steal from your employer, to cut corners when no one is looking, and to lie to cover it up. You're tempted to join in with the chorus of complainers who always focus on the negatives and are never satisfied.

Before being faced with these temptations, you must use gratitude as an antidote for the poisons of greed, covetousness, and bitterness. David certainly knew this and included so many songs of praise within the Psalms. "It is good to give thanks to the Lord, And to sing praises to Your name, O Most High" (Psalm 92:1). He knew that we must focus on what we have, not what we wish we had. Our human nature is such that we're always prone to compare and stare across the fence at our neighbor's greener grass. But have you ever noticed that once you attain what you wanted so badly, your satisfaction doesn't last long at all? You're on to the next thing, and the next, and soon you're on a treadmill of conditional living with the carrot always dangling in front of you but never in your possession.

True contentment appreciates each day. The Lord's mercies are new every morning and we must focus on the numerous blessings that cover us. Did you have a warm place to sleep last night? Do you have your health? A place to live? Food to eat? Clothes to wear? Do you have a job? We can so easily take so much for granted and lose sight of what we have to the point where our present gifts seem invisible to us because we're always looking ahead. Instead we must practice contentment with what the Lord gives us, trusting that His provision is sufficient for this day. Like Paul we learn to say, "I have learned in whatever state I'm in to be content" (Philippians 4:11).

PRIDE WILL SLIDE

Gratitude also helps stave off another potential infectious disease in your hostile work environment—pride. Your ego and overappreciation of your own abilities can so easily get in the way of performing your job in a godly manner. Both superiority and inferiority can exploit your self-pride and contaminate you with either an elevated sense of your own importance or an undervalued sense of yourself. If you keep your identity positively centered on who you are in Christ, then you will be able to resist those moments in the workday when you might feel arrogant or contemptuous about yourself. Being grateful for who you are as a daughter or son of the King allows you to remain humble.

It's tempting to succumb to pride as you ascend the corporate ladder. But remember that when pride takes a ride you're bound to slide! Others are telling you how great you are, what a fabulous job you're doing, and the promotions and deals serve as evidence to prove it. But no matter how important others tell you that you are, you must remain humble. Otherwise, you're setting yourself up for an incredible fall. More than ever, you must remain focused on your Christian identity and not on the title on your business card. Don't become pretentious as you advance. Keep it humble. Stay modest. Give credit to others as much as is due. Pride and ego inflation lead to posturing, grandstanding, and people pleasing instead of God pleasing.

Remember that David knew he had been anointed to be king long before he started the job. He was forced to be patient and wait on the Lord's timing rather than assume the prize and force things into motion. David understood that his ascent was the result of God's blessing and not his own doing. Similarly, Joseph, whose rise to power we explored earlier, also was forced to wait on the Lord and to know that God's faithfulness would fuel his recognition and leadership, not his own abilities.

You must also make sure that you don't fish for compliments to bolster your self-esteem. Don't use false modesty and fake humility to solicit praise from others. If you struggle with low self-esteem, don't make the work environment your source of countering this affliction. Others will sense your weakness and take advantage of your desire for praise and need for attention. So often our coworkers and employers will treat us in the way that we allow them to treat us. Do your best to keep these relationships polite, professional, and pleasant.

If you feel unrecognized and unrewarded for your efforts, you must once again remember Who you're doing it for. You must trust that He will bless you according to His abundance in His time. When others ignore you, diss you, unfairly criti-cize your job performance, or backstab your character, you must not succumb to believing any of these lies from the enemy. Their words are simply the devil's fiery darts trying to scorch through your defenses. Pray for the protection of your Father and remember your true identity.

ARMOR ALL

As we've seen, numerous toxins abound in our work environ-ment and these can easily invade our own attitudes, thoughts, and behaviors. Foremost, we must stay focused on the spiritual battle at hand and prepare for it adequately by putting on the armor of our faith that Paul describes in his letter to the Eph-esians:

> Finally, my brethren, be strong in the Lord and in the power of His might. Put on the whole armor of God, that you may be able to stand against the wiles of the devil.
>
> For we do not wrestle against flesh and blood, but against principalities, against powers, against the rulers of the darkness of this age, against spiritual hosts of wickedness in the heavenly places.
>
> Therefore take up the whole armor of God, that you may be able to withstand in the evil day, and having done all, to stand.

Stand therefore, having girded your waist with truth, having put on the breastplate of righteousness;

and having shod your feet with the preparation of the gospel of peace;

above all, taking the shield of faith with which you will be able to quench all the fiery darts of the wicked one.

And take the helmet of salvation, and the sword of the Spirit, which is the word of God.

(EPHESIANS 6:10–17)

As you put on your armor each day, ask the Lord to bless you for His battle that day. You might pray the following prayer to get you started: "Heavenly Father and King of All Creation, I thank You for allowing me to work in my present position. I praise You for all the blessings You've given me in my life and ask that I would continue to appreciate the abundance I have in my life. As I suit up for work this day, please protect me, empower me, use me, and bless me as I go into the battlefield against the enemy. May I remain focused on You and use Your Word and Your power to shield myself from the contaminants of hostility, workaholism, bitterness, pride, and greed that may come my way. I rest in the victory secured for me in Christ Jesus! In His majestic name I pray, Amen."

When you go into your workplace armed with this prayer and these truths that we've discussed, you embrace who you are in Christ and you refuse to take the devil into you. Ships sail on water, but if the water gets in, even a battleship will sink!

Go through the waters of your work environment, but don't let the "water" contaminate you. You can easily get caught up in what transpires around you and allow it to victimize you. Much of who you are is defined by the time invested in what you do, so guard your heart and your spirit from "workplace contamination."

Be realistic in expecting what the job will deliver. Keep your focus on why you were sent there. Keep your armor on and claim the victory that Jesus has already prepared for you. Proclaim the truth, "I am the person for this job, devil, and you are not going to run me out of here. I am going to run you out of here!"

Be strong in the Lord and flourish!

INCREASE YOUR CAPACITY TO WORK WITH DIFFICULT PERSONALITIES

MANY believers I know hope to work in full-time ministry one day. Their goal is to work in an environment where there's praise music playing and coworkers praying. With Scripture verses neatly calligraphied on wall plaques and crosses around every neck, these people imagine such a place as holy and peaceful. They believe that once they have a job in a Christian environment that one of their primary sources of hostility—getting along with their coworkers—will disappear.

While I wish that this were the case, I'm afraid that until our Lord comes back we will always have some level of difficulty relating to coworkers, whether Christian or not. Believing that ministry work is one harmonious worship service is indeed a mistake. I have traveled the length and breadth of this nation and most of the world, worked with Christians and non-Christians alike and believe me, there is very little difference in how personnel operate under pressure. Christian or not, most people react similarly in hostile work environments. You see the mind is not new. It is constantly being renewed—even the minds of Christians. This doesn't mean that they are not saved, but it may mean that they are not as mature as they should be. Disagreements, arguments, conflicts, tempers, grudges, and gossip often affect churches and ministry organizations as much as any other office. Pettiness, greed, ambition, and favoritism all creep in as the enemy fires his darts and hopes to create a flame. We would like to think that as believers our faith allows us to work without strain or tension, but that is simply not the case. We are not perfect, and so if we are going to survive our hostile work environments then we must increase our capacity to work with difficult personalities, regardless of the kind of workplace in which we're placed.

ACT LIKE A PRO

I'm afraid that as Christians we are often contributing more to the problems in office relationships than to their solutions. Christians can be the most selective and discriminatory group of people on the face of the earth, and as a result rob themselves of rich exposure and growth. Many times we feel obligated to show our faith by criticizing people with whom we work rather than just loving them and seeking God for a chance to say something helpful and encouraging. Often we are a great witness but we ruin our testimony because the sinner knows that while we witness about Christ we do not act very Christian. Others observe our behavior and our testimony suffers because of poor work ethics, long breaks, reading the Bible on company time, talking on the phone for hours with our friend, and so on. But the very worst thing is that we often alienate ourselves as an elite group of people and leave others feeling somehow less than us. This draws a negative contrast when we compare our behavior to Jesus, who mingled with the masses and rubbed elbows with rich and poor, high and low, different ethnic groups, and outcasts. He seemed especially adept at reaching out to those who the rest of society often looked down upon—the prostitutes, the tax collectors, the lepers.

Yet too often we're trying to fit in and connect with others similar to us. We like to put people in our world into two boxes: the ones we like and the ones we don't. We use the same tools in the workplace for people evaluation that we do in our personal lives. We deem people either good or bad, black or white, on our side or against us. While our personal preference plays into who we choose as friends and who we like to hang with, you must realize yet another important distinction about your job. The workplace is not an appropriate setting for en-forcing your own set of rules on who counts and who doesn't, on who matters and who doesn't, on who you might hang out with or totally avoid. Brothers and sisters, this is so dangerous!

First of all, work is not the setting for establishing relation-ships. Save that for the country club, the ladies' home fellow-ship, the church picnic, or the golf course. A workplace, especially today, will include many ethnic groups, cultures, reli-gions, and even sexual orientations. You have to be able to work with people you might not relate to personally. You have to have the flexibility to work with a diversified age range and per-sonality span. Working in a diversified place requires wisdom. An employee must develop a professional attitude, one in which personal opinions of any individual do not come into play.

How can your attitude toward different or even difficult personalities affect your performance quality? One of my fa-vorite expressions of truth, and you may have heard me say this before, is: He'll use the devil to bless you!

Might I remind you that God used a raven—a dirty bird—to free the prophet Elijah? God used Pharaoh to fund the build-ing of the tabernacle. The wealth of Egypt established the provision of God in the wilderness. Nehemiah built the walls of Jerusalem with the money of a heathen King. Those who you shun because you don't like them may just be the conduit to your good fortune. By avoiding them, you may unwittingly block a blessing that God has stored up for you. Your tendency to alienate certain people in the workplace can actually handicap you in life, resources, and finances. Nobody can escape working with difficult people, but God wants His people to grow in the midst of negativity, not be "sucked into" it. If you allow God to enlarge your understanding of people and work relationships, you may be ready to have Him enlarge your territory. God won't give you something you are not ready to handle, but He does want to expose you to greater things and greater ways of managing life.

David had that sought-after ability to work effectively with difficult people. It doesn't get much more challenging than working with someone who has an "evil spirit troubling him." Saul was that challenge for David, yet David blessed Saul. In the beginning of David's time with Saul, David had favor, but later on, Saul sought after David to kill him. *But David never changed his strategy.* David stayed in the house because he knew the anointing and blessing was his in the house. Because of David's conduct and the way he wisely handled the situation, he was in line for promotion and ended up "owning" the house.

We need to apply the wisdom of the Bible to contemporary situations. God's principles are ageless. David didn't limit himself and he surely didn't limit God! David knew that people are made up of "vessels of honor" and "vessels of dishonor." Getting his eyes off of people, being neither impressed nor depressed by them, afforded him unlimited opportunities because he freed them up to be used by God. Learn to work with difficult people; the very challenge you have today may be the one who tomorrow determines your promotion. And conversely, sweet

Sally may be the very one who informs the boss if you walk in six seconds late one morning. Learn to remain not aloof but professional, and depend on God to reward you.

EYES ON THE PRIZE

How do you cultivate a professional attitude? Begin by keeping your eyes on your objective. Are you selling windows? Then don't walk into someone's living room and offer them unsolicited advice about their living room décor. Limit yourself to what you are called to do. People can be easily offended, and by speaking about areas outside your expertise—what your customer has solicited your help in—you can jeopardize your opportunity to make a sale. Learn to appreciate people, even those you don't like. Customers are not friends; friends are friends. Appreciate your customer because hopefully he has the money to buy what you are selling. Place value on people and respect them even if your personal feelings are conflicting! This requires focus. Remember the blessing of the Lord is not predicated upon personality.

David had little in common with Saul, yet David stayed obedient to God and responded as God instructed him to. David's prophecy was fulfilled because he accepted the training program and the sometimes hazardous road it took in order to grab hold of what God had for him. David could have thrown up his hands for more reasons than we will probably ever experience, but David had his eyes on something down the road, not the brief comfort he could gain if God had altered his temporary conditions. God is able to do "exceedingly, abundantly" more than we can imagine, so risking that because we don't like someone's hairdo or voice patterns is a foolish price to pay.

Another way to maintain your professionalism is to treat everyone fairly and equally. You will naturally find some customers, coworkers, and administrators easier to work with than others. You may have some personal interests in common with some and not others. But if you show favoritism by only being kind and respectful to those you like, then you are in for trouble—if not now then down the road. You will need to work with those people who aren't your favorites somewhere along the way. And they will remember your nasty attitude and not be particularly inclined to help out. You may even need a favor from them, assistance that goes beyond what they are required to provide you. People, especially coworkers, can be here today and gone tomorrow; placing unmerited value on temporary encounters can rob us of permanent blessing.

Acting like a professional also requires that you discipline yourself and stay focused on the work. In order to get what God has for you, self-control will have to be manifest in your thought life and in your conduct. When Saul started throwing javelins at David, David ducked and kept on serving. While he was clearly innocent of any wrongdoing, David defended himself without becoming defensive in his attitude. Always having to talk back or speak up could position you to get hit square in the head! Do it God's way, like David did; humble yourself and as you bow low before Him, you are safe in His shadow as the darts are boomeranging around you!

Try not to take things personally, even when unhappy coworkers intend them to hurt you. Remember that you are so much more than just an office manager, a temp worker, a high school science teacher, an accounts manager, or an advertising executive. Work to live, don't live to work! You must learn to let go of grudges and to set aside past histories with some of your coworkers. When you find your emotions flaring and you're tempted to react, stop yourself and remember what's really going on: you're in the midst of a battle and the first shots have just been fired. This is the time to say a silent prayer, remember your true calling, and respond with patience and a professionalism that will astound those around you. If you are not easily ruffled by difficult personalities, then you will increase your ability to remain cool in the heat of the battle. Your decisions will be more objective and levelheaded and you will be able to keep the work goals in mind as opposed to operating out of your personal moods and preferences.

OIL AND WATER

In developing a professional and Christ-centered attitude toward those difficult personalities in your workplace, it's helpful to understand some of the dynamics that can contribute to interpersonal friction on the job. Like trying to mix oil and water by shaking the bottle again and again, many Christians believe that if they just act nice around those difficult personalities that eventually those people will change and become nice too. But "nice" doesn't always cut it, especially when you use it to avoid confrontation and direct communication. Oil and water will never mix. True kindness isn't afraid to look someone in the eye and tell them the truth, even if we know that this isn't what they would like to hear. You will garner much more respect for yourself and your beliefs if you act on kindness and honesty rather than "niceness."

Other problems stem from lack of clarity regarding job descriptions and divisions of labor. "I didn't do that report—I thought that was part of your job. Aren't you assigned to the marketing department?" "Did the boss ask me to complete this project or are you going to do it?" Tense conversations like these shouldn't be avoided, but you should work to keep tempers cool, attitudes professional, and communication lines open. These are the weapons for the warfare you face. Unfortunately, school doesn't teach conflict resolution; churches don't either. Often we do not learn it at home, so we step into workplaces either unwilling to confront, or—at the other extreme—unwilling to resolve the conflicts. But the conflict must be resolved! If it is not attended to, it will metastasize like cancer, spreading its debris and manifesting as obnoxious attitudes and discontentment. Effective conflict resolution is a key ability of someone with good character. And good character is an invaluable commodity in life—and especially in the workplace. Good character is more than great morals. It is possible to be morally upstanding and still not exhibit the character that makes you an asset to an employer and a recipient of promotion.

Do you have the ability to resolve conflicts, simply and efficiently, seeking out the common good? When you are confronted, can you hear what the other party is saying instead of talking over the person so you can debate and defend yourself? Can you forgive the one you confronted or who confronted you so that you do not pollute the environment with hostility? If you can't, your gifting, education, or skill may have taken you to a level in life and given you an opportunity, but your poor character will ultimately destroy everything you've worked so hard to accomplish.

There may be times when your best efforts at maintaining cordial relationships with coworkers are met by an inscrutable wall of resistance. When reconciliation seems difficult, jealousy may be the underlying combustible that fuels some of those fiery relationships. Misguided admiration can manifest as jealous behavior in some people. The colleague who starts rumors about you may be envious of your gifts, your education, or your looks. The manager who seeks to undermine you at the board meeting may be jealous of your relationship with the boss. Those personalities who seem most antagonistic around you may secretly admire you and resent themselves for being different.

If you sense that jealousy is an issue with someone, you

might make an extra effort at praising their strengths or commending them for work well done. I'm not advocating flattery or false praise here; if your words come across as insincere, then that will only escalate the problem. But this is a great opportunity to subtly minister to someone by building up their self-confidence. Plus, by pointing out their good qualities you will often disarm the competitive edge the relationship is taking. There have been times when I have been criticized, and my first reaction was to lash out and retaliate. But I have learned that often this criticism is a by-product of someone feeling left out and my best defense is to include them and thus defuse the situation.

Immaturity and foolishness can also heighten the tension when you interact with difficult personalities. This is especially true if you are a type A personality, a straight-ahead working person who is results-oriented. It may really frustrate you as you work with people who come to the workplace seeking fraternity and frivolity. You are working hard to display your maturity, to utilize self-control to keep the work goals in mind, when these people act silly, childish, and unfocused. They don't want to hear what you have to say: "The way of a fool is right in his own eyes, but he who heeds counsel is wise" (Proverbs 12:15).

You know the type. These people seem to ignore deadlines, don't carry their weight, and find every chance imaginable to spend time on trivia while you are focused on triumph. They have a joke for every occasion, have some personal commentary about every current event or media story, and want to celebrate every holiday from Christmas to Columbus Day with an office party or potluck luncheon. These are the ones who forward countless e-mail quizzes, humorous stories, and personal photos to everyone in the office. Many of these people mean well but expect to be entertained, amused, and enjoyed by others on the job. They are looking for a family in their workplace, and as we've seen, this is simply not the place to build your community.

In fact, these kinds of difficult personalities can be some of the most challenging to work with because you are forced to challenge their basic philosophy about the purpose of employment. This will require extreme diplomacy on your part. And you may have to settle for small inroads—"Marcy, our system server isn't able to handle personal e-mails in addition to all of our customer orders"—and allow your example, and hopefully the example of other more mature office mates, to set the standard. If their foolish behavior becomes too disruptive, you may need to confront it directly or discuss it with your supervisor. You don't want to be a "tattletale," but you also want to be honest about why the work isn't getting done.

As surprising as it may be, other believers in your hostile work environment can often pose challenges that you would not expect. Instead of being each other's prayer partner or ally, you instead become competitive and combative, bringing out the worst in each other. It can almost become a contest to see who is more "Christian." You make comments about each other's churches, pastors, or ministries. You provide unsolicited commentary on how the other believer should be responding to someone else. You treat them as the less mature, weaker brother or sister. Obviously, this kind of display is rarely genuine Christianity and instead amounts to self-righteousness. When these moments occur with other believers in your workplace, you must stop and realize what the enemy is about.

Think about it for a moment: if the devil can create dissention and division among the believers in a given workplace, then he's killed two birds with one stone. He has not only diluted the potential power that you could all experience as a united energy cell of God's children, he's also used you to undermine your witness to nonbelievers. You must realize that the enemy wants to prevent you from supporting and allying with other Christians in the workplace. If he can shoot you down with "friendly fire" from one of God's own, then he has gained another foothold in winning this particular battle. I'm not advocating that you have to be best friends or attend the same church with your believing coworkers; I simply encourage you not to fall prey to the enemy's snares that will divide you and create a negative impression.

LEARNING AND GROWING

When we learn to get along with all the various types of people in our workplace, particularly those who we find so challenging, there is a double benefit. Not only will our work go smoother, but we will also become better, stronger men and women. You might begin to understand from this that part of your job responsibilities include being able to work well with people, and often these are people who are quite different from you. Most of us gravitate to people who think like we do, however I have learned that the best teams are not comprised of people who perform the same functions; great teams require diverse gifting. It is an amazing asset when you can work with various types of persons and build teamwork and fraternity for eight hours a day. It will cause you to have a lifetime of results. It is a win-win deal.

So often God uses trials with these difficult persons to build our character and to increase our own store of maturity and wisdom. By attempting to avoid or ignore those who are so different from ourselves, we are often avoiding the very training that God has provided for us to advance to the next level. Because regardless of the kind of work you're doing, we all have to relate to other people. So be grateful when difficult personalities create challenges in your workplace and know that God is indeed equipping you for your future.

What are some of the benefits of learning to work with difficult personalities? What can we learn from working with people so different from ourselves? Certainly the individual lessons and equipping will vary from person to person and situation to situation. However, there are some general areas that we can expect to grow in as we interact with people who are tempera-

mental, immature, jealous, overly competitive, or even prejudiced against us.

One of the first lessons we may be forced to learn involves
the true meaning of acceptance and tolerance. Just because
someone is different from us in their appearance, lifestyle, reli-
gion, political affiliation, or personal beliefs does not mean that
we should dismiss them or think them inferior to ourselves.
You don't want to be judged and dismissed for your color, culture, or countenance, do you? Then don't assume to prejudge
others in similar fashion.

One problem that believers often grapple with when becoming more accepting and tolerant of diverse people involves
this very notion of judgment. Since God's Word is very clear
about us not becoming like those of the world in their sinful
practices, we often are tempted to think we are better than
they are (a sin in itself!). Or on the other hand, we fear that if
we accept these people, then we are endorsing or accepting
their sin. The truth lies in remaining respectful and accepting
of other people in the same way that Jesus was respectful and
accepting of those with whom He interacted. Whether it was
racial differences (Samaritans and Gentiles), lifestyle differences (the woman at the well, Zaccheus the tax collector), or
class differences (Nichodemus, the rich young ruler), Jesus
managed to love these people as they were while inspiring
them to a higher standard.

It's easy to say "love the sinner and hate the sin," but living it
out requires practice and reliance on your Father's guidance. You

don't have to relinquish your beliefs about sin in order to work alongside sinners. You can work alongside someone who's having an affair without having one yourself. We ourselves were once sinners, now saved only by the grace of God and the cleansing sacrifice of His Son. Avoid the traps of self-righteousness and act with humility and grace when you encounter those people whose differences make you uncomfortable. Learn from them as much as possible. Allow them to dispel your preconceptions and stereotypes. Learn to see them as individuals and not as a collection of demographic differences.

FRUITS OF OUR LABOR

As we grow in tolerance and acceptance, we will naturally increase in patience and compassion as well. These qualities are natural fruits of learning to see people as individuals. The more we realize that despite certain differences we are all human, all created by our Father in His image, then we become free to focus on our similarities. When we don't understand someone else's motives and personalities, it's easy to assume the worst of them and become very impatient. Why can't they work their scheduled shift? When are they going to turn in their section of the quarterly report? What's taking them so long to report back to the team leader? While these may be valid questions, there are often legitimate reasons, at least in the other folks' minds, regarding their delays or sense of timing.

Communication and trust go a long way toward increasing our patience and understanding of those who do things differently than we do. Perhaps they can't arrange child care for their scheduled shift and need to trade with someone else. Maybe they are waiting on data from another coworker before they can crunch their numbers and complete their section of the quarterly report. Maybe they're frustrated by the criticism leveled at them by the team leader without any constructive suggestions for improvement. I often use the power of deduction to find a way to remove anything that may be hindering them from performing well. I will often say, "I know there has to be something in your way; it is not like you to lag behind on this." When you phrase it like this, it sounds like a compliment more than a reprimand and it gets results. You may also say, "Is there anything I can put in place to help this not to happen again or make it easier for you to handle?" Try to think toward removing any obstacle that would give them a valid reason to fail.

You can become a conduit of communication and compassion by simply asking the right questions. Too often we're afraid to ask someone what the problem is. Or when we do ask, we do it in such a way that it only increases the fear and hostility the other party is experiencing. If we ask with kindness, or at least in a pleasant, objective manner, then we free the other person to tell the truth. Instead of them making up excuses, we can have an honest dialogue about what needs to happen to get the job done or the problem solved. Such an exchange builds trust between the two of you, which increases the likelihood of better communication and more efficient problem solving the next time. It puts you on the same team rather than making you opponents. Poor productivity, not the individual, is the enemy.

As a good communicator, you will also have to learn how to compromise. Now, I don't advocate compromising your Christian values, convictions, or beliefs. However, you must realize that being a Christian doesn't give you the right to impose your belief system on others no matter how right we think that we are. Many times we do not understand this and it leads to frustration, or even termination.

The kind of compromise that's required when dealing with difficult personalities refers to each person letting go of something they'd like in order to accomplish what is needed. You may prefer to have an office assignment completed in a certain way by a certain time, but in order to accommodate the differences in someone else, you may have to set aside your preferences and find a reasonable solution in between. You shouldn't become a doormat and let others walk on you and have their way, but you should realize when you're being stubborn or inflexible.

Learning to compromise will help make you a better negotiator. And if there's one thing that most of us have realized already, it's that negotiation is one of the cornerstones of the working world. From the time we interview for a position or submit an application, we begin to negotiate. When do you need me to start versus when would I like to start? How much can you pay me compared to the amount I need? How many hours do you need me in the office each week instead of working from my home? As we continue on the job and begin completing assignments and solving problems, we learn that it usually involves a system of give-and-take, of back-and-forth, of checks and balances.

This is where you must keep the large objectives in mind and not become blindsided by the momentary obstacle. You may win your particular battle, but will it cost you so much that it affects your witness or your work? Will it make others see *you* as the difficult personality in the workplace? This is often how the enemy will bait you. He seduces you into looking like the villain by encouraging you to poorly manage a situation in your workplace. I feel that God is moving many of us into positions of promotion. The question is, are you ready for this next level of responsibility? I am not asking are you competent and capable of doing the job. I am hopefully broadening your understanding that managing different people is a part of increasing your borders and setting yourself up for increase. It is more involved than an increase in pay. Generally an increase in pay often comes with an increase in pressure and responsibility. Winning the verbal battle and showing everyone how vicious you can be is not nearly as important as persevering respect and accomplishing goals. Remember that the weapons of our warfare are not carnal but mighty through God. Allow God's purposes to guide you as you negotiate and communicate with people of many different agendas.

One of the ways I dispel stress in my own life is to keep a sense of humor. I have to occasionally remind myself that not everything is a code-blue, red-alert, crisis. Remembering not to use unnecessary force helps me. I am also learning that sometimes maintaining a sense of humor can make me more effective. A happy person will always get more done, get more sales than his oh-so-serious counterpart. Being joyful can make you laugh all the way to the bank. Who would you rather buy a car from, a stressed-out, verbally abusive person or someone whose company you enjoy? Who would you rather work for or around? Someone who is congenial or someone who is always moaning and complaining about what ought to be done? "He will yet fill your mouth with laughter and your lips with shouts of joy" (Job 8:21). Finding the humor in a tense situation can often ease the tight vise of conflict and unknot the cords of discord. "A cheerful heart is good medicine" (Proverbs 17:21).

However, I should add two warnings about humor in the workplace. First, always make sure that your humor is at no one else's expense. Avoid making jokes about things that others might actually be secretly sensitive about. Weight, bad hairdos, and cheating husbands might make everyone else laugh, but to many people this is not funny. No one likes to be the butt of the joke or to be made fun of. You must be careful with teasing someone else, making sure that their personality can handle the humor. It is always wise to let the joke be on you. You know you are not going to offend yourself! Second, you must remember that timing is everything and ensure that your comedy contributes to the solution so desperately needed rather than becoming another obstacle to its completion. Sarcasm and mockery are always inappropriate. Keep the humor clean and wholesome and use it as a tool to build unity and maintain the big picture.

GROW BY GRACE

You may never receive a diploma in diplomacy, but you can learn what God wants to teach you by sticking it out and not giving up when difficult personalities add hostility to your work environment. Every relationship, every path we cross, and every conversation we have can ultimately be used by Him to further His purposes. We mustn't dismiss or ignore those who seem different from us. We must endeavor to love others within our workplace, trusting that God will shine through us and allow us to interact with those who we find most challenging.

As you look around you at the assortment of personalities and temperaments in your workplace, I encourage you to thank God for each of them and ask for His guidance in how you relate to each one. You may even want to name them and discuss with your Father why it's such a challenge to get along with them. The following prayer might help get you started:

"Almighty God, I am so blessed to be in my present position and I thank You for all the abundant ways that You continue to use and to bless me in this job. I'm grateful for each and every one of the difficult personalities in my office, even the ones I don't particularly like or understand. Thank You for Fred in accounting. I don't like his temper but I pray that I could learn to not fear him and grow in my ability to communicate with him. And thanks for Betty in the cube next to mine. She talks all the time and always wants to socialize instead of working, but I know she's just looking for connection. Help me to be kind to her while maintaining the focus on the work before us. Give me Your words the next time that I have to ask her to end her conversation and focus on work. And there's Karen, and Tim, and my boss, Reggie. I know I'm the person for this job! So I pray that I might learn how to be a better witness not just in the words I say but the way I do business and the attuitude with which I serve others around me. Thank You, Jesus! Amen."

WHERE YOU ARE
IS NOT WHERE YOU
ARE GOING!

I can still remember working in the summer on my grand-mother's farm. Early in the morning before the sun had peeked above the Mississippi clay, she would arise and start her day. She seemed determined to gather the eggs from the henhouse, feed the mule, and milk the cow while the day was yawning and the sun was breaking into the sky. The smell of freshly turned dirt still fills my nose. As I think of it, I can see my granny with her big hat on her head and her brightly colored muumuu-style dress moving out through the wooden screen door, across the cow pasture, dropping through the gate beyond the barn and into the fields, where newly developed peas awaited her thickly callused hands. I was basically a city boy playing country, running behind her, having more fun than really working. But to this day I can still remember how hard she worked. And although at the time I was more interested in my own antics than the tasks at hand, her example made a lasting impact on me.

My grandmother could really work. Sometimes even now, if I tilt my head and close my eyes, I can almost hear her raspy voice—somewhat like my own—singing hymns and spiritual songs in the damp morning air as she bent over the fields gathering peas for the day's picking. She and my great aunts would work until the sun made it too hot to work outside any longer. Her crackling voice never faltered as she belted out the hymn while bending over the soil. Maybe if she had lived in more modern times she would have had a Walkman attached to her as she moved. Maybe she would have played some contemporary tune in her ears as the battery-operated machine whizzed and purred, giving music to the work she had engaged in before the day was fully started. But none of that was possible back then. It was just her own aging voice carried in the wind. That was the only jukebox we had to listen to as she worked and sweated over the fields while I worthlessly ran behind making noise and playing as a child. It almost seemed that her own song fueled Grandmother's pace. I know she thought I was just in the way, but I learned from her to sing while I work.

No, I am not suggesting that you need to literally start

singing at the computer. I am pointing out that though my grandmother was working, she was content. She had a full day's work ahead of her, but still she sang out joyfully. The fact is, my grandmother was peaceful while progressive. She hadn't yet finished her work, but she was happy while she worked on. This is an art that seems to escape this generation today. They are either so goal-oriented that they are miserable, always delaying any sense of satiety for the sweet by and by, or worse still, they are satisfied to have an empty barrel and sit in a field complacently wasting time without being motivated to achieve the goals that they set out to accomplish.

My grandmother, probably without even realizing it, taught me to be assertive enough to maintain a progressive gait, but also to be happy even though I had not attained my ultimate goal. Now I would like to think that my grandma, in her big flowered dress, had the franchise on such philosophy, but that simply isn't true. In reality she was only doing what Paul teaches in his epistle. She had learned whatever state she was in, therewith to be content. She was contented. But even though she was contented, she remained progressive. My grandmother sung her way through college, although she didn't get to go until she was a full-grown woman. In between chores, washing and ironing for the neighbors, she earned her degree and ended up teaching children until she retired. Her wash pan full of peas turned into a library full of books because she knew how to enjoy where she was and still reach for her goals.

Had she allowed the racist times she lived in there in Mississippi to deter her, she would have given up and settled for less than what was possible for her. Had she allowed the heavy work schedule she endured to deter her, she would have decided it was too late in life to make a second attempt. But Granny knew where she was . . . and she also never forgot where she was going.

Now I know few of us are picking peas anymore, but many of us may be working a job that is as difficult and hot, uncomfortable and menial as that might have seemed to her at the time. But the art to not losing your personal momentum and keeping your heart motivated is to do what you are doing well, but keep where you are going in mind. I call this singing while you work.

DEEP ROOTS

But how do you deal with your present position when you know you have somewhere much greater waiting for you? This type of perseverance requires that you remain motivated. And I'm talking about the long-term, here-for-the-long-haul kind of motivation—the kind that has deep roots and feeds on springs of Living Water so that when the storms and droughts and winters come, you have the nourishment you need to stay alive and thrive.

David knew this kind of motivation and describes it in the very first Psalm:

Blessed is the man
Who walks not in the counsel of th
Nor stands in the path of sinners,
Nor sits in the seat of the scornful;
But his delight is in the law of the Lord
And in His law he meditates day and night.
He shall be like a tree
Planted by the rivers of water,
That brings forth its fruit in its season,
Whose leaf also shall not wither;
And whatever he does shall prosper.

(PSALM 1:1–3)

If we consider the many turns, twists, and trials that David endured over the course of his lifetime, then it's clear that the only way he endured was through his reliance on God and his pursuit of His calling. Even when David failed—and he made many mistakes, from adultery to murder to ignoring his children—he returned to his roots and remembered that where he was, no matter how bleak it might seem, was not where he was going.

What's the secret to this kind of motivation? I believe that it must be grounded in hope first. In the twenty-seventh division of Psalms, David says he would have fainted had he not believed to see the goodness of the Lord in the land of the living. This is hope to me. It is not enough to have a hope for heaven while one accepts the present hell as inevitable. If one ccepts the present as the final prognosis then defeat is the terrible consequence of a flawed mentality. Like my ancestors before me who survived many plights and perils, I too must overcome obstacles with optimism and forge ahead singing my way into destiny, redefining barriers, moving the split-rail fences that man has erected, threatening to keep me living in the prison of preconceived ideas. These are the sociological ideas that have locked many of us into the mediocre while we are called to the extraordinary.

> For which cause we faint not; but though our outward man perish, yet the inward man is renewed day by day.
>
> For our light affliction, which is but for a moment, worketh for us a far more exceeding and eternal weight of glory;
>
> While we look not at the things which are seen, but at the things which are not seen: for the things which are seen are temporal; but the things which are not seen are eternal.
>
> (2 COR 4:16–18, KJV)

One of the greatest challenges you will face is to avoid the temptation to lose heart and become discouraged while you proceed toward your goal. Particularly in the workplace, it's so tempting to lose heart and simply detach and go through the motions like some kind of zombie, doing our job but disconnected from our larger purpose. In those moments when we're feeling underappreciated, overworked, and in between a rock and a hard place, that is when we must remember the singing of our grandparents, who knew that just around the corner or way up north there was a brighter tomorrow that would never be realized if they were to accept the present darkness as a death sentence.

Now you don't have to share my ancestors to share the principles that made them strong. They were people who, like Paul says, endured the light afflictions for the weightier glory. They were people who ignored the present inconvenience for the ultimate hope of changing their reality with the relentless tenacity that dares to sing in the rising sun of limited access and dismal statistics. Hope springs eternal in the soul of every believer who will use his faith to get up on his feet. I believe faith will work if you work it. Work your faith and move ahead. Nothing can stop you if you just believe.

I know that it feels so hard in the moment, so aggravating and annoying, so painful and purposeless at times. But in light of what's taking place in the spiritual realm, invisible though it may be to our mortal eyes, we know that all things are working together for good for us that have been called by Him.

GROWING PAINS

As we set our sights on the future and remind ourselves that we have not been abandoned in our job, we must also be prepared to experience the discomfort of growing pains. When children are growing, they sometimes complain about a sore limb or pain in their joints. If there is not an injury or discernible cause for the pain, then we often tell them that they are just experiencing growing pains. I know I said this to my children. I think that I said this because this is what my parents told me whenever I complained as a child about minor aches and pains that had no apparent cause.

Whether children really experience growing pains or not, we do certainly experience growing pains in our careers. It's the tension caused by taking care of details on one end of a trip even as we prepare for our arrival in a new destination. A frequent cause of growing pains is doubt over new responsibilities or projects. You may feel overwhelmed by a fear of failure that looms high above you like a boulder waiting to fall from the sky. You may believe that you will suddenly be exposed as a fake, a phony, someone pretending to be good at this job rather than someone capable of doing it well. Sometimes these fears eclipse your thinking so much that you lose sight of where you're going and become content to stay where you are. You're so afraid to risk more that it's easier, no matter how frustrating or painful, to remain where you are.

These feelings are totally natural and to be expected. As you begin to exercise talents that were dormant, or as you step up into a new role, you may be unsure of your abilities. But you need to have confidence—in yourself and in your Lord who put you in your current position. You will need to rely on prayer more than ever and on the support and encouragement of family and friends outside your workplace. Try not to express your doubts and fears in the workplace if possible. Let your fears keep you humble and dependent on the Lord, but not paralyzed.

Sometimes it is not wise to express your goals either. Joseph made that mistake and found out that his brothers were not happy for him, nor did they share his enthusiasm for his dreams. Sometimes we have to keep quiet and grow silently, biting our lips and enduring some pains, knowing that this too shall pass.

Another source of growing pains that many of us have experienced is overextending ourselves. We simply take on too much too soon and find ourselves buried beneath mounds of paper, past-due deadlines, overdrawn accounts, and weary bodies. These eager beavers try to embrace the future and fail to realize that you can have a vision but that it doesn't mean that you can walk into it today. Most visions require timing and patience. Patiently waiting is what Grandma taught me. She also taught me to work while I waited. But the thing so many of us forget is that we cannot get to tomorrow today.

> Then the LORD answered me and said:
> Write the vision
> And make it plain upon tablets,
> That he may run that readeth it.
> For the vision is yet for an appoi/
> But at the end it will speak, and
> Though it tarries, wait for it;

Because it will surely come,
It will not tarry.
Behold the proud,
His soul is not upright in him;
But the just shall live by his faith.

(HABAKKUK 2:2–4)

We're multitasking to the point of never focusing on any one item, giving it our singular time and attention, because there's so much that we feel we must do. While I certainly advocate multitasking within reason, you must also make sure that you leave time to focus without distraction on your highest priorities. Don't expect yourself to be a machine. Many of us are anxious about our goals. But when we are, we are not being fueled by our vision; we're actually stressed by them. You cannot manage what hasn't happened yet. If it is your time to pick peas don't try to study while you are picking peas. You will likely not do either very well. I've met many people who are really great visionaries but lack the skills to manage the vision against their current obligations. Grandma had to pick what was ripe. You cannot let what God has given you spoil on the vine while you chase what tomorrow will bring.

Maybe a good place to start is managing your time. Leave yourself some time for working on what is real while planning on what is forthcoming. Your vision may be real to you, but cannot get to tomorrow while you are wrestling with today. In fact, in order to be ready for the challenge of the future, remember to reserve some time to rest so that when it does happen you are not too exhausted to reap the harvest that God has promised you. You need to rest up for the promise. To fail to do so will cause you to ruin great opportunities because you underestimated what it would take out of you to get to the next destination.

Don't overlook the basics like food, sleep, and exercise. Some people take better care of their dogs and cats than they do of themselves! Keep in mind that while you think you're saving time by skipping lunch to work on that report, when you start to crash in mid-afternoon because your body has no energy, then you'll pay a much heftier time penalty than if you had taken thirty minutes and eaten a healthy meal. The same goes for sleep and for exercise. When urgent projects demand attention and new requirements necessitate changes in your schedule, I'm afraid that too often we view sleep and exercise as luxuries and not necessities. If we are truly going to grow into the next level of our calling, then we must not overlook our own needs. Some things must truly come first. Yes, there is a time to work late or pull an all-nighter, but this must not become a lifestyle habit. If you want to reach your next destination, then you must plan accordingly by taking good care of yourself.

TIME FLIES

One of the reasons that so many people forget this commandment or struggle with its truth is because they feel like there's
such a huge gap between their present job location and ultimate career destination. "Yes, I'd like to be a teacher, but that
means I'd have to go back to school and finish my degree. That
would take years!" "Sure, I'd love to switch careers but this job
has security; I don't know if I could afford to take the risk." "It
would be fun to try and market my own jewelry that I've been
making as a hobby, but I don't know how to get started."

On and on the excuses pile up like dirty dishes next to a
sink. It feels like it would take too long, cost too much, require
too many sacrifices to jump from point A to point B. Whether
it's going back to school or starting your own home business,
the temptation is to always put it off until another time. Maybe
when my wife gets a job, maybe when the kids are grown,
maybe when I retire. But you must realize that time is our most
precious commodity and we must make the most of it each and
every day.

TAKE ONE STEP AT A TIME

So how do we overcome these obstacles and begin moving
toward our next destination? My answer is simple and perhaps

obvious but please read it carefully: *We must form a large goal and take small steps.* If you want to go back to school and graduate with your degree so that you can switch careers, then make that diploma one rung on your ladder. Set this as your first ring surrounding the bull's-eye for which you're ultimately aiming. From there, find out what your options are regarding how to go back to school so it would work with your other commitments to job and family. Break this into steps and spend a few minutes each day following through. You might begin by requesting a transcript and seeing which courses you already have completed and which ones you need to complete the degree. You might request catalogs from the universities and community colleges in your area. Based on their expense, course offerings, times of classes, financial aid offered, and the recommendation of others who have attended there, you might choose which school best fits your needs. Then you can make an appointment with an admissions counselor, who can help you plan a schedule that will allow you to complete your degree.

While it's tempting to think that the amount of time required is too long, you need to keep in mind that those days, weeks, and years will pass whether you are pursuing your goal or not. So often God wants us to show up for duty as He calls us and leave the provisions—including time, money, and material resources—to Him. If we do our part, God is faithful to enable us to follow through on the execution of His plan.

I'm reminded of a friend who is training to run a marathon,

something that seems unthinkable to many of us. So I asked him, "How in the world do you motivate yourself to run twenty-six miles? That must seem so daunting! Do you ever want to quit?" He smiled sheepishly and replied, "All the time! I'm always tempted to quit, especially when I think about how far I am from the finish line. The first few miles are easy. But then I get tired just thinking about how much farther I still have to go. So then I promise myself that I'll run the next mile before deciding whether to go on. Sometimes I'm so tired or struggling so much to persevere that I promise myself only the next hundred yards. Then another hundred yards. Pretty soon another mile has gone by. I have to break the distance down into manageable pieces, and learn how to play mind games with myself so that I'll keep going."

We can learn from my friend's strategy. Break the distance down into a few steps at a time. You don't have to complete eighteen college courses today; you only have to do your homework for the one class you're taking this semester. You don't have to sell your homemade beauty products to Oprah or be on QVC today; you only have to offer them to a couple of girlfriends at church who have expressed interest in them. You don't have to develop a new marketing paradigm for your software; you only need to do some research and make a few notes about how others have marketed their software. You need to quit focusing on the huge steps required to arrive at your next level and simply take each step one at a time.

So if the gulf seems too wide and the current seems to be

moving too fast between where you stand now and the other side of the river, ask Him to help you begin building the bridge you need to cross. The other bank may look too far away and there may not be any earthly means to cross that raging water, but God does not operate by earthly means. Don't be discouraged just because you don't know how you're going to get there. Just focus on the large goal of building that bridge and take the first small step of getting started.

DON'T THINK YOU'VE ARRIVED

Why do so many talented, successful people suddenly crash and burn in their careers? Whether as the result of their personal lifestyle or their professional judgment, they seem to be an up-and-comer and then they nosedive into obscurity. Certainly there are numerous factors that play into the complex equation of one's career success or failure, but I'm convinced that a major contributor has to do with how one views success.

If we measure success in material ways, then we will likely come to a point of being successful if we're willing to work hard enough. Some people know they've made it when they're no longer in debt, when they can pay cash for an expensive sports car, when they can afford designer clothes in all the exclusive shops. But then what? Once they can do these things does that mean there's nothing else for them to work toward, nowhere greater for them to go? Now that kind of thinking is a recipe for disaster. I'm not saying that you shouldn't enjoy the fruits of your labor and the blessings that God bestows upon you. But if material possessions are your only benchmark for success, then you will likely be disappointed and then flounder to find meaning in your work.

One of the greatest barriers of pursuing the next-level destination that God has for you is to settle for the one where you are located presently. Either your imagination is limited or else the enemy has used fear—of either success or failure—to clip your wings. Don't ever think you've arrived! This is one of the lies that the enemy loves to plant in our thoughts. Because if he can convince us that we've arrived, then we won't need to work so hard, we won't need to keep growing and stretching, we won't need to rely on God as much.

The dangers with thinking you've arrived are life-threatening. You become so comfortable that you don't realize that you're still in the midst of a battle zone. It's as if you've found a little cottage on the beach where you're content to remain, not realizing that the beach is Normandy on D day! Don't be tempted by luxury and material affluence to abandon the larger Kingdom purposes for which you were born. You can certainly enjoy the benefits of financial success without making them an idol that eclipses your vision of where God wants to take you.

Another problem with thinking you've arrived is that you lose touch with those who are not on your same playing field. Suddenly you feel like you're above those who aren't as blessed as you have been. Your attitude becomes one of subtle superiority as you patronize those who continue to work hard and pursue their dreams. No matter how successful you become, brothers and sisters, never forget where you came from! God has blessed me in tremendous ways that I could never have predicted and imagined when I started out as a preacher of His Word in a small storefront church in West Virginia. All I knew was that He had called me to speak for Him in this place and I wanted to serve Him this way. There were times when I didn't know how we would pay the electric bill to keep the church warm for Sunday service in winter. There were times when I worked two jobs to supplement my preaching. I didn't always know how long it would take to get to "better days," but I never stopped believing that they were ahead. That is why I am telling you it doesn't matter where you start. It matters where you finish. Now I have come a long way from where I was, but I am a still a work in progress and so are you. Keep reading. Keep looking. And keep on building. God is not finished blessing either you or I, and as we go, we will encourage one another. You may not be there yet, but I have a feeling you are closer today than you have ever been before.

So as you experience success along your career path and enjoy the blessings that the Lord provides for you, do not lose sight of the ultimate destination. Remain humble, knowing that there is still much to learn, many people to encounter, and problems to be solved. Remember that your journey is ongoing—where you are is not where you are going, even when where you are is a place you'd like to remain.

PAST TENSE

A major barrier to our view of where God wants to lead us occurs when we are so fixated on our past that we cannot turn our heads and see the future. Like Lot's wife turning to watch Sodom and Gomorrah burn and becoming a block of salt, we must resist the temptation to linger in the quicksand of past mistakes, either our own or other people's. If we wallow in regrets and "what ifs" from the past, we are basically limiting God's ability to redeem our mistakes. If we wallow in past hurts and the injuries inflicted by others, then we become victims who blame others for our lack of contentment in our lives. In either case, when we live in the past we refuse to take responsibility for our lives and to trust in God's sovereignty and goodness. I know it can be hard to see when such horrendous things happened to you in the past: childhood abuse, failed marriages, drug addiction, jail sentences, and family betrayals. However, when we become bogged down in the past, we miss what God has for us in the present and its connection to our future.

Many people get stuck in the past because they feel like it's too late in their lives and their careers to change. But the truth is that it's never too late to allow God to use you and move you forward on your journey. As we've seen with Joseph and with David, God redeems the evil inflicted upon us by others as well as the poor decisions that we ourselves make. How much sweeter is the Prodigal's love for the Father because he knows what it's like to be alone in a foreign land! How much dearer is the gift of His Grace because we're aware of how much we've hurt others? How much richer is His comfort and peace because we know what it's like to be injured by the selfishness of others?

It's never too late to change. I just read a story about an eighty-three-year-old cancer survivor who has just completed her first exercise video for folks over eighty! God delights in transforming our weakness into His strength. He can produce treasure from what we've discarded as trash. Just as He transformed the kid into a king in David's life, God is always there for you, encouraging, reminding, and challenging you to be all that you can be. Take it from my pea-picking grandma: God will take you from picking peas to college degrees. Keep a positive attitude. Sing when you can, hum when you must, but keep moving down the row. Who knows what God has in store for you around the next bend?

If you've backslidden and taken a detour from the path that you know He wants you to follow, then now is the time to return to His highway. Leave your past behind and look at where you're heading. Move out of the past tense and into the future perfect. Now get busy digging down into your personal deposit and see what God has stored up for you!

COMMENCEMENT EXERCISES

Did you ever notice that when you finish school, whether it is high school or college, the institution conducts "commencement exercises"? These include the traditional ceremony where degrees are conferred on graduates and outstanding students and accomplishments are recognized. Other events may celebrate the occasion as well. I was always surprised and a little confused as a kid that this benchmark was called "commencement," meaning the beginning, when it sure seemed to me that it was the end of a lot of hard work. Twelve years of math, science, literature, geography, history, and other subjects. And then additional years of harder, more complex subjects for college.

But as I grew older, I realized that every completion of a goal is the beginning of the next goal. While it was true that the new graduates had just completed their programs and degrees, this was only in preparation for something greater—living out their lives with integrity and passion. Some variation of this message is usually delivered by a commencement speaker, an honored guest of the school, who attempts to congratulate and motivate the new graduates as they prepare for the next phase of their lives. So think of this as my commencement address for you, a graduate of the school of life, a lifelong student of His Word.

Never forget that you are anointed for the job at hand.

God knows the plans He has for you, plans for a future and a hope. He has placed rich deposits of gifts and talents in you, and the enemy wants to keep you from that destiny! God wants to pull out of you what He has hidden down inside you! If things are difficult, it's because God is stretching you, pulling from within to empower you to do something you've never done, see someone you've never seen, touch something you've never touched! If it's easy, you've mastered it; now it's time to lean toward the finish! Have you ever wondered why you are not dead yet? The devil could have killed you long ago, but God still has an unended story that you alone can finish. Maybe you are not even healthy, but you're still alive because God is not finished with your biography.

Some of you come to church every week and shout and dance and still hate your life! Church is not an escape from trouble or a drug where you can get a Sunday fix. I have learned that many people who were once suffering from addictive behavior now have substituted their addiction with a church addiction. You don't want your faith or your preacher to make you high. What you want is your faith to fuel your life and empower you for what you do outside of the church all week long.

Just to emphasize how important it is for you to get this message into your spirit, let's do a little arithmetic to see how much of your life is tied up in your job and its accompanying efforts. If you average eight hours on the job, one hour to and one hour from, and then one hour each evening detoxing from your daytime environment, that's approximately four thousand job-related hours of your life each year. In light of the truth that time is all we're given to work with, that's too much time to do anything that will not be effective and eternally productive. Use your time wisely.

And regarding the destination where you're headed, God wants you to enjoy the journey! He wants you to live with expectancy, joy, and peace. He didn't create you to be miserable and therefore make everyone around you miserable! The devil wants you to hate your life and go to sleep and have nightmares about it. He is trying to steal the joy from your heart. But God has another plan. The Lord gave you your job as a way of meeting your needs, and Satan would have you hate the resource God is using at this time to bless you. Don't allow the enemy to rob your joy. Even though you may be very good or even excellent at what you do, some people will not want you on staff if, with your expertise, you usher in confusion and a rotten atmosphere. Most people who do that do not realize that they can be right about what they said but wrong about how they said it. The right motives with the wrong methods will not equal success. Attitude is critical. Remember, and say it with me, "I am the man for the job! I am the woman for the job!"

Please allow me to close our little commencement service with a prayer:

"Our Heavenly Father, we are so grateful for who You have created us to be and where You are taking us. Please allow us to live out of the rich Hope that You provide for us through Your sovereignty, goodness, and love. Bind the enemy from discouraging us with his weapons of doubt, fear, arrogance, and affluence. Help us to formulate a plan to pursue those large goals that You set before us while showing us the baby steps that we need to take today in pursuit of these goals. Remind us that where we are is not where we are going and bless us with Your joy and peace as we continue on our journey. In the Precious Name of Jesus, Amen!"

EIGHTH COMMANDMENT:

ACHIEVE OPTIMAL
RESULTS WITH MINIMAL
CONFUSION

A S I reflect upon the many challenges of the workplace and the numerous obstacles that often clutter the path to success, I find that none is more dangerous than confusion. Like a thick fog swirling down halls and into offices and cubicles, confusion is one of the enemy's most subtle and devious tricks. When we're confused, we lose focus, miscommunicate with one another, duplicate responsibilities while allowing others to go undone, and watch our momentum come grinding to a screeching halt.

Confusion often originates with lack of communication as people begin to make assumptions, to second-guess one another, and to act out of fear and self-interest. Instead of focusing on our primary tasks, we become distracted, disturbed, and derailed from our principal mission. We feel overwhelmed and wonder if we can ever catch up at work or if our work even matters. The enemy loves it when this happens because then he can undermine our mission more effectively.

SLOW BURN

When we become confused, overworked, and frustrated by feelings of futility long enough, we eventually get caught up in the spiral of overextension and burnout. Many times I've observed talented men and women quit their jobs due to stress or become sidelined by illness or injury. While they clearly have the talent, capability, and calling to perform their jobs with excellence, it's just as apparent that they wore themselves so thin that the fabric of their spirit has experienced a tear. As my father used to say, "You can work a good horse to death!"

In conversations with some of these people, I'm continually surprised that these individuals often blame themselves and resent the fact that their minds and bodies were not able to carry such a burdensome load. It's almost as if they expect themselves to perform like machines, on command, always consistent and productive. These folks are usually gifted multitaskers who thrive on checking items off their lists and succeeding in a variety of venues. It is true that multitasking is often a good way to accomplish many things at once, which can be a good way to achieve optimal results from your investment. However, when multitaskers begin to lose focus, when they can no longer respond to every e-mail, return every phone call, write every report, and contact every customer, they feel like absolute failures. They're always expecting more and more from themselves. They literally want to be able to accomplish as many projects as possible at one time.

Now there's nothing wrong with challenging yourself and striving toward the next level of performance. But if you don't learn your limitations and respect your boundaries, you will not only lose momentum but you will lose perspective, no longer able to see the path clearly, no longer enjoying the journey. Confusion then increases like a gathering storm, growing in its power, obscuring your vision, and blurring your purpose for being in your position. When you attempt to do too much, or expend energy doing the wrong tasks for your gifts, then you add to the confusion that often reigns in a hostile work environment. In order to keep your vision in place, to stay focused on what you do best, and to achieve the optimal results, you must begin by learning your limits.

SPEED LIMITS

Although many drivers on our highways and interstates seem to believe that the posted speed limits are suggestions rather than enforceable laws, it's helpful to remember why they are there. It's not to slow us down just so that we're always crawling along below our vehicle's horsepower capability. No, the speed limit is there to protect us from ourselves and from each other. And most of us have observed, if not experienced, the consequences when the speed limit is not obeyed. Drivers lose control and spin out of control, crashing into telephone poles, the median, or other cars. When a collision occurs, not only is the driver sometimes injured and sidetracked from the journey, but the collateral damage that accompanies his crash often takes others down with him.

Just as speed limits exist for good reasons that need to be respected and practiced consistently, so we must discover our own work "speed limit" and honor it as well. Any time someone exceeds their limitations on the job and then crashes, their wound ripples throughout the entire organization. Are you trying to take work home, staying up late after the kids have gone to bed and your spouse is fast asleep? Are you skipping meals so that you can get caught up on the paperwork that seems to replenish itself faster than kudzu growing along a hillside? Have you become accustomed to driving to meetings, checking messages on your BlackBerry, drinking a cup of coffee, and taking a call on your cell phone all at once? Not only is this insane for you personally, but it's incredibly dangerous to yourself and others when you attempt to run a portable office while driving sixty-five miles per hour down the freeway!

While there are some seasons that are busier than others—

occasionally tremendous opportunities come along and projects require extra time and attention—you must not expect yourself to always travel at warp speed. You are a human being, mortal and fragile, with physical, mental, emotional, and spiritual needs. You aren't a robot, a computer, or an engine that can be operated with the flip of a switch. Even for these mechanical devices, if you don't keep them fueled and maintained, they will eventually fail to operate properly.

How do you discover and maintain your speed limit? You begin by knowing yourself inside and out. I recommend that you pay close attention to your body's signals as well as your emotional responses to the demands that you place on yourself in the workplace. When your body is tired to the point of distraction, then you need to rest. When your feelings refuse to be ignored, then you need to express yourself in some appropriate ways.

Too often we ignore our bodies' needs and the screaming voice of our emotions inside us. I'm always amazed when I hear about some world leader, celebrity, or sports star who collapses at a public event or performance because they had forgotten to eat and drink! We must not ignore our bodies' need for food, for rest, for touch, and for exercise.

Now I know it's tempting to say, "Bishop Jakes, I'm always tired! I stand all day and my feet hurt and my back aches and my head is pounding." We've all had times when we have to work even though we're tired or sick, perhaps because we're working double shifts or holding down two jobs to make ends meet. But even in the midst of these situations, I maintain that you still have to find a way to get some rest and take care of your body. If you're constantly ignoring your body's aches and pains, eating out of the vending machine, running on caffeine and adrenaline, then eventually your body is going to let you know that it can't operate this way for very long. You will get sick and be forced to slow down and be taken care of by medical professionals since you obviously won't take care of yourself.

Similarly, we've all experienced times when our feelings are bouncing around like a pinball inside us even though we're forced to maintain that calm and cool composure for our meeting with a client or conversation with our boss. We want to scream out, "I hate this place! I'm so much more talented than you know!" Or maybe our feelings aren't even related to our job at all; other events and relationships in our lives are distracting us and preoccupying our thoughts. We think to ourselves, "I'm forced to smile and nod during this presentation while my marriage is falling apart, my child is being sentenced for drug possession, and my mother is dying of cancer." These are the times when we have to make a distinction between our personal and professional lives. As sympathetic as coworkers or customers may be to our plight, they can't comfort or care for us like friends and family can. Our client doesn't really want to know that we're afraid our spouse is having an affair. Your office mate may not know how to respond to the news that you've found a lump in your breast.

So we must learn to tend to our emotional needs apart from our professional responsibilities. Whether that's through a prayer partner, a regular coffee time with a friend, or conversations with a counselor or pastor, you must find a way to let your feelings out. Certainly taking them to the Lord in prayer and pouring out your concerns to Him remains the best way since He is the one Who cares about you most.

Knowing your speed limits also allows you to know when you've been going too fast for too long. Like a premier Indy racing car, you can only make so many laps around the track before you need a pit stop to refuel, replenish, and restore your energy. Although we've discussed in other chapters the necessity of taking good care of yourself, I hope you can appreciate how *not* taking care of yourself has a domino effect on your ability to perform in the workplace. If you overwork without replenishing your storehouse, then eventually you will become less and less effective at what you do.

Making your health and well-being a priority may feel selfish at times, but it actually allows you to be more productive. When you're rested, you will not only have more energy and stamina, but more creativity as well. Simply by eating well, sleeping enough, exercising, and taking regular vacations you can increase your productivity considerably.

ONE-TRACK MIND

Once you've discovered your speed limits, then you want to make sure you remain on the same road that you started on.

When we go too fast, we can easily become lost, pass the intersection where we intended to turn, or speed into uncharted territory. In order to achieve optimal results with minimal confusion, we must remain focused on the job for which we were hired. It can be tempting to want to do others' jobs for them, to increase our load of responsibilities, or to diverge and perform other tasks for which we may be well suited. Yet when we take these detours, we often increase the confusion. We were hired for one job, and when we start doing other tasks or taking on different roles, we lose our ability to get that one job done. We must cultivate a one-track mind by constantly making sure that our main work priorities remain the same.

Jesus never lost sight of the reason that His Father sent Him to live among us. Or, if we reconsider David and the reason he's "hired" by Saul, we see that he excelled in his ability to play the harp, the job at hand. And that's why he gets the position.

> And Saul's servants said unto him, Behold now, an evil spirit from God troubleth thee.
>
> Let our lord now command thy servants, which are before thee, to seek out a man, who is a cunning player on a harp: and it shall come to pass, when the evil spirit from God is upon thee, that he shall play with his hand, and thou shalt be well.
>
> And Saul said unto his servants, Provide me now a man that can play well, and bring him to me.

Then answered one of the servants, and said, Behold, I have seen a son of Jesse the Bethlehemite, that is cunning in playing, and a mighty valiant man, and a man of war, and prudent in matters, and a comely person, and the LORD is with him.

Wherefore Saul sent messengers unto Jesse, and said, Send me David thy son, which is with the sheep."

(I SAMUEL 16:15–19, KJV)

The job description goes out and David has what is needed. He's "cunning in playing" and knows that's what's required of him.

Similarly, the strengths and attributes that get you hired should be the ones that you exercise most in your current position. Although, like David, you may possess numerous other talents and abilities, you must trust that God will use those at a later time. Stick with your present mission and make it your consistent focus, especially when you are tempted to take on more.

Remembering your primary purpose in the workplace may also require that you say no to certain requests made of you, perhaps even after you've indicated an initial willingness to do the task. You may so enjoy pleasing others that it's incredibly difficult for you to say no and risk their disappointment, displeasure, or dislike. But you must remember that you can't please everyone; you can only please the Only One. When you keep your eyes fixed on God and your ears attuned to His voice, then you free yourself up from having to always please others and seek their affirmation. You can risk disappointing them without always second-guessing the consequences.

LET GO AND LET OTHERS

In order to avoid the confusion of the workplace and maintain your primary mission, you will most likely need to find new ways of operating. Instead of doing too much at once and spreading yourself too thin, you will need to learn how to function as part of a team. You may have to speak up more and let others know that you can't do everything by yourself, even though you have been trying and even wish that you could. Those of us who tend to be control freaks have a real problem letting go of some of the details and delegating to others or working as a team. But if we insist on doing everything ourselves, soon we won't be able to do anything!

No, we must learn to delegate areas outside of our primary focus to others. Delegation is often humbling to people who are multitalented and used to excelling in a variety of different roles. Yet they inevitably learn that it's difficult to offer your very best in more than a couple of areas at one time. If you are truly going to fulfill your unique and particular purpose for being in your present position, then you must learn to let go of some things and let others help you. Humility only reminds us of our humanity and God's sovereignty, so don't miss the opportunity to be blessed by Him through others by being too proud to ask for help.

If delegation is one of the most effective ways to prevent burnout and to alleviate stress in your work life, then you will be forced to decide what to delegate. This requires an examination of what's required of you versus what's produced, what's invested, and what's returned. You may be nowhere close to burnout but simply wish to be more productive and effective in executing your job responsibilities. Maybe you're not overextending yourself but you're just plain frustrated by the impasses and logjams in your work environment. I believe we must begin by assessing this important ratio between what we expend and what we produce.

Achieving optimal results with minimal confusion requires what business leaders call a "cost-benefit analysis." This is just a fancy way of saying that they weigh the cost and requirements of a new position, product, or project against the benefits and positive outcomes produced by that same new item. How effectively are you spending your time in the workplace? Do you spend thirty hours a week attending to minutiae that only contributes to 2 percent of your company's revenue while only devoting ten hours a week to projects that generate 40 percent of your company's profit? Now unless this is the balance required and explained in your job description, most of us would find this incredibly counterproductive. We need to devote most of our time and energy to those areas of greatest importance.

I encourage you to take a few minutes and jot down the tasks you consistently perform on the job and the amount of time each requires. Are you balancing the significance of the task with the amount of time needed to complete it? Can you expend your energy in more effective, productive measures? Use this list as a guideline for reconfiguring how you invest yourself in your goals and responsibilities.

Once you have observed areas that need change, then your goal becomes clearer. Perhaps you feel like you spend most of your workday returning e-mails and phone calls rather than performing your primary work task. Your solution may be as simple as setting aside a regular block of time at the beginning and end of each workday when you will only answer e-mails. Otherwise, you turn off that function on your computer and focus on your primary goal. You can quit worrying about how many e-mails you have and stop interrupting your other responsibilities because you know that you will be attending to this correspondence at set times of your day.

SOAR IN STRENGTH

Often there are simple solutions that we can employ to maximize our effectiveness. I believe that in many cases we spend too much time trying to compensate for our weaknesses rather than capitalizing on our strengths. For example, a good friend of mine is a talented musician, vocalist, and record producer.

He knows how to fill every note of a song with passion and every word of the lyrics with emotion. He knows how to assemble just the right people to perform on an album to achieve the highest quality product. However, for several years he flirted with burnout and became creatively blocked, which led to severe depression.

One day as he was discussing his work with me, I realized why he was likely struggling so much with his career: he was focusing most of his time on contracts, accounting, royalty statements, and legal matters. He was spending too little of his time writing music, performing his songs, and recording studio sets with other artists. In other words, the administrative aspects of his business had superseded his area of giftedness where his passions lie. He could easily afford to hire a business manager and attorney to oversee all the business-related concerns and free himself up to focus on using his creativity to do what he does best. After reorganizing his office and hiring others who were gifted in his areas of weakness, my friend is more fulfilled, and more successful, than ever before.

Many times optimal effort for minimal confusion requires this kind of delegation to those whose gifts complement your own. You may want to appear as if you can do it all and don't need support or help, but you are mistaken. Everyone needs support! You know the old saying, "Behind every successful man is a good woman"? Well, the reverse is certainly true as well, "Behind every successful woman is a good man"! In fact, I would maintain that behind every successful person in the workplace is a team of talented individuals supplementing, complementing, and implementing on his or her behalf.

Now we might not all be so fortunate as to work in a position that utilizes all of our gifts. But we should at least be moving in that direction. If you know that you're a creative person with a talent for design and the visual arts, and you are currently frustrated by your accounting job, then it's time to reconsider your career goals. If you love to solve problems when your computer breaks down but you're currently working as a cake decorator, then it's time for you as well to step back and reassess.

You may not be able to make a living at your primary passion at present, and so you're working in an unrelated field to bring home the bacon and keep food on the table. But your sights must remain set on following God's calling and pursuing your dreams with the gifts with which He has equipped you. Perhaps you know that you are anointed for a position that apparently has nothing to do with your primary gifts. If this is the case, then you simply have to trust that God is equipping you for something that's on the horizon.

CHANGE OF TUNE

Much of the time, however, we are placed in our present position so that we can do what we do best, even if that gift doesn't seem to fit the job description for our position. Simply performing the thing you do best is often the most effective way to solve a problem. Let's look at the example set by our biblical work model, David. What did David do when Saul got an evil spirit? He played the harp! David was truly anointed and knew that God had placed him there to be part of the solution, not to add to the confusion by compounding the problem. He didn't act like a fool and cause confusion; he simply picked up the harp and changed the atmosphere!

How have you responded to the atmosphere in your work environment? How can you create a change of tune in your workplace by utilizing your gifts? I doubt you will be called to play your favorite musical instrument like David, but you never know. My guess is that more likely you will find ways to break the tension with hostile coworkers through your excellent communication skills, your expertise as a negotiator, or your disarming use of humor when tempers are flaring.

Your ability to change the hostile atmosphere might be the result of something as simple as complimenting a coworker on a task well done. Perhaps you rearranged the office space or reconfigured the cubicles so that it was more functional as well as more pleasing to the eye. When hostilities increase and problems escalate, don't be afraid to change the environment before tackling the issue at hand. David wasn't supposed to counsel Saul about his sinful mistakes or to cast out the evil that was afflicting the king's spirit. No, David was there to offer comfort and solace in the midst of a problem that wasn't his to solve. He didn't try to do more than he was called to do.

David knew that an anointing brings peace, not confusion. Nobody wants to hire people or even be around people who usher in confusion. If a choir director sees problems in the musical arrangement and order of the songs and only criticizes and editorializes about the problem, he doesn't solve the problem or facilitate its solution. If a salesman observes an issue with distribution, but only complains to his customers about it, he not only doesn't solve one problem but creates another one.

In the midst of his on-the-job confusion, what did David do? He played the harp. God has given us an effective tool to remain in an atmosphere without becoming contaminated by the hostilities of others. With our anointing and giftedness we can remain insulated from the environment and even change its atmosphere. It's because of that posture of detachment from the environment that we can remain under the shadow of the Almighty and because of that bring peace, truth, and hope to those who need it most.

EXPERT WITNESS

Isn't it amazing how simply the anointed can accomplish the work of God? It looks effortless for the expert. Some people sit down at the piano with starched shirts and ringed fingers that dance over the keys, making music that invites angels. The pianist rises to bow and the audience applauds vigorously in appreciation of a flawless performance that was as smooth as silk.

The pianist's shirt is still dry, his hair is still in place even though he bowed five times, and his appearance and conduct are as composed as when he first sat down and flipped his coat. You get the picture.

On the other hand, I can play the piano, but when I am finished, no one is giving me an ovation! By the time I'm finished playing, I'm sweating from head to toe and I may have missed a couple of notes. You see, I am not effectively anointed to play the piano. You know the surest indication of all? I haven't moved the audience. Anointed people move people; they are effective at bringing change. There's nothing to parallel the connection between God, the person playing the instrument, singing, or preaching, and the people they are sent to inspire!

And God has instilled that gift in every single person! Jesus said, "As the Father has sent me, so send I you!" You are sent to that very environment that needs a light, a smile, a word of encouragement, a good reliable worker, a prayer warrior who prays while typing. We are His expert witnesses! By exercising our gifts as He has uniquely created us, we glorify and honor Him, our Creator. There are no restrictions or limitations on how God can use His children. And the thrill is incomparable. It gives the individual a special sense of belonging to God and service to Jesus, the One Who dwelt among us serving. When we are doing what He created us to do, we feel His pleasure in our service.

God is so creative and delights in diversity. Don't stay stuck in the lie that you have to act like someone else or do what someone else is doing in order to be effective in the Kingdom. Anointing is not a style; it's an enablement of God to be effective. Styles come and go, but the message remains the same throughout the centuries of time. We are simply carriers of truth, hoping that what we give is highly contagious!

I met a woman long ago who shared what God had given her early in her walk with Him. She related that it had saved her from missing precious moments from God through people she would otherwise have disregarded. In the vision, He showed her three cups. The first cup was an enamel camping mug. It had nicks and stains in it and was so beat up it could have been thrown out. The second cup was an ordinary kitchen mug used for daily cups of coffee. It was nothing special, just a plain brown mug. It had nothing to distinguish it from any other the manufacturer had produced in mass scale. The third was a fine china cup, sitting daintily upon a china saucer. With delicate patterned flowers and leaves, its beauty was extraordinary and made it appear to be one of a kind, surely a collector's item. The camping mug may have been found with a bag lady, the kitchen cup in any ordinary American home, the china cup in a special high-profile setting with many admirers. In the midst of these three very different cups, God had simply spoken and said, "I will give you water in any one of these. Just recognize that it's Me. And drink."

Each of us has a specific style; God created all the styles. It's the anointing that delivers to the hopeless what God wants to bring through our presence. No matter what your cup may look like, you contain His Living Water that satisfies the desperate thirst of those around you. Don't be afraid or ashamed to offer water because of the way your cup appears.

RIGHT ON TIME

Yet another key to achieving optimal results with minimal confusion is to cultivate a sense of Divine timing. Worrying about what might happen or what could happen only drains your energy and frightens others. Instead, you must trust that God has equipped you to solve problems and handle situations as they arise. You may not know what the solution to a problem is until the time arrives when you are faced with it. As we've seen with David, he was forced to rely on God's timing for his Divine appointment with the throne of Israel. Even though he had already experienced God's anointing, he was forced to wait, even after he came into the palace. If he had entered into Saul's presence and announced that he was taking over, David would have diverged from God's plan.

You may have heard the expression "God may not arrive when you want Him to but He's always on time!" By staying in close proximity to the Word and within earshot of God's voice, we seize opportunities when they present themselves rather than forcing a solution that's premature. I encourage you to act at His prompting without questioning the logic or rationale behind it. When He asks you to play your harp, you can trust that He has a reason!

As you reflect on other more individual and personal ways that you can achieve optimal results with minimal confusion, I encourage you to ask for God's guidance and direction. You might find the following prayer helpful in making your request:

"Dear Lord, I am so thankful for the unique gifts that You have instilled inside of me. I'm grateful for the way I'm wonderfully and fearfully made in Your image. Please use me according to Your purposes in the position where You have placed me. Allow me to be an instrument of Your peace and sovereignty as I go into my workplace and encounter the confusion and hostility of others. Like David picking up his harp and playing for Saul, may I have the clarity of vision to see what You would have me do when evil strikes. Allow me to be an expert witness for who You are and what You are about. May I be a faithful steward of all the resources to which I am entrusted. Strengthen my resolve to be the person for this job! In Jesus's name I pray, Amen."

NINTH COMMANDMENT:

DO NOT PLEDGE ALLEGIANCE TO CLIQUES AND GROUPS!

A skimpily clad young woman is forced to leave the exotic location where she's been competing because her teammates feel threatened by her intelligence. An Ivy League–educated entrepreneur in an Armani suit snaps his briefcase closed and dejectedly rises from the conference table after hearing that he's been fired. These scenarios may not be typical in your workplace, but they definitely reveal the consequences of committing to cliques and groups.

From viewing the many reality-type television shows, we've become accustomed to watching one person ally with another in order to push their common adversary off the island or out of the boardroom. Friendships are forged, secret pacts made, and necessary alliances formed as each individual jockeys for position, power, and prestige. However, only one of them can win the prize, and this fact means that sometime during the game players must betray those alliances and friendships. Deception and deceit become as much survival tools as a compass and matches. Loyalty, trust, and integrity go by the wayside. Each player wants to win the game and is willing to do whatever it takes to survive and be the last man or woman standing, no matter who they have to climb over to get there. As the commercial for one reality show preaches, "Make friends, make alliances, but trust no one!"

We are presumably entertained by such antics, but I suspect that we're so engaged by these complex webs of team dynamics and individual personalities because we've experienced them ourselves. While our experience hasn't likely been as concentrated or as public as the situations on reality TV shows, they are probably just as intense, hurtful, and surprising. Coworkers we thought were our friends suddenly stab us in the back. Bosses who tell us we do a good job one week hand us a pink slip the next. Supervisors who force us to work overtime brazenly take credit for the report we compiled. Sadly enough, we become accustomed to office politics and the intricacies of relationships in the workplace. This reality makes it all the more essential that believers should not pledge allegiance to cliques and groups in their place of employment.

SOUL SURVIVOR

It would be nice to think that Christians would be unaware of and shocked by such harmful practices. Unfortunately and ashamedly, though, the church is one of the most common environments for cliques. Certain ladies look down upon other women who are perceived to not be at their same social standing because of the way they dress. Members of the choir regard nonmembers as unworthy of their time. Men and women in leadership let the power go to their heads and don't want to interface with those they promised to shepherd and serve. Thank the Lord this isn't always the case, but you know what I mean if you've been in the church for very long!

Perhaps this tendency serves as one of the reasons so many Christians are attracted to clique formation. We like the safety of being with others like ourselves who won't threaten us or intimidate us with their differences. As long as we're with others who think and act like we expect them to, we won't be surprised or required to change. If we keep the group homogenous, we can rest in the reputation of the group. Maybe it's human nature to crave this kind of consistency, but it's also incredibly dangerous.

This pattern, which offers a false sense of security, is often transferred to the workplace, where cliques and groups can create damage and dissension, resulting in a horrific atmosphere for workers. People are no longer perceived as individuals but as on this person's side or in that person's corner. Perhaps some of you all share George's beliefs about the way certain tasks should be completed. Maybe the marketing team thinks they're more indispensable than the accounting department. Suddenly every word or action has political and personal ramifications. The workplace becomes a chessboard of pawns moving around for the kings and queens. Some groups support this person today but not tomorrow. If a person isn't willing to jump on the group bandwagon, she is perceived as a threat and bad-mouthed.

Such factions and cliques become nothing more than hubs for gossip, affairs, backbiting, and every imaginable mess that man can create. The enemy is busy on your work site stirring up unhealthy relationships so that he can hinder and limit your usefulness. If he can preoccupy as many believers as possible by having them focus on the latest rumor about Susie over in the mail room or where the boss was seen last night with his secretary, then those Christians forget why they are there in the first place. The enemy disarms us by tempting us with the security of the group and approval of others. We become more concerned with making sure we continue to be liked by the members of the clique rather than fulfilling our Kingdom purposes and pleasing our Creator.

But we must outsmart that devil! If you want to be a soul survivor, then you must be as innocent as a dove and as shrewd as a serpent in your dealings with others. If you are currently in a work environment where hobnobbing with a certain group has become habitual, then find a new work pattern. While it may feel good to belong, such a group can easily serve as a snare to involve you in arenas where God doesn't really want you to be so connected. Members of the group might pressure you to accept their judgment concerning other coworkers even though your experience doesn't support that judgment. Soon the clique is moving from the office to happy hour at the local bar. Or you find someone hitting on you because of the close-knit nature of the group dynamics.

Like Joseph running out of the grasp of Potiphar's wife, break free as quick as you can! Don't flirt with disaster. Certainly I realize that you can't become a loner and simply avoid people in your workplace. You will usually be forced to work with others and to be part of certain teams or groups at work. Most jobs require some level of group involvement, team building, or committee work. But the kind of cliques and groups I'm talking about here are identifiable because of their exclusive and exclusionary mind-set. Their energy feeds on conformity and compliance instead of being open to others and stimulated by diversity. Most cliques develop an elitist attitude that makes it difficult for nonmembers to interact with them. Outsiders tend to be vilified as either inferior and unworthy of being part of the group or as threatening to the power dynamics within the group. In either case it's incredibly unhealthy and creates a minefield of potential explosions on the job site.

GROUP THINK

Since the security of the group is so important, there's pressure to conform and experience "group think." This is the term that psychologists and sociologists use to describe the way people yield their individual preferences and responsibilities to the opinions and ideas of the majority. It's what happens when you really want Italian food but everyone else in your group wants to go out for Chinese, so you agree or keep quiet about your preference. In the workplace, you may believe that completing a project requires additional help from subcontractors while the majority of group members want to keep it internal. You don't want to create waves so you keep it to yourself.

While compromise and negotiation are essential when dealing with others on the job, group think can have devastating consequences. The crowd mentality can have you suddenly doing things you never thought you'd do—whether it's loosening your values and morals because everyone else is or remaining silent while the group berates and bullies someone else.

Group think is what allows a mugging to take place on a busy city corner—people see or hear the crime being committed but don't want to get involved. They assume that since there are so many other people around that someone else has called the police and the paramedics. Many experts claim that statistically you stand a better chance of being assisted if there's only one person present when you experience a heart attack than if there are a dozen close by. This same phenomenon may contribute to your participation or silence regarding a practice that you know is wrong. You know that cheating the government or lying to customers is wrong, but you don't want to be the whistle-blower. You may even fear being turned upon by other group members if you stand up for what is right. You could risk losing your job.

Nevertheless, it is a risk worth taking when your core convictions are at stake. Certainly you must pick which battles to fight in order to win the war, but some offenses should be intolerable. For example, following the majority and allowing it to dictate your individual behavior goes a long way in contributing to racism and sexism, age discrimination, and the prejudiced behavior that accompanies them. Cliques gain their strength from shutting out others who are different. And no matter how you slice that, that's discrimination. If you weren't allowed to join a country club because of the color of your skin, your sex, or your ethnic background, you'd undoubtedly be hurt and outraged. How different is that from not inviting someone to sit with you in the company cafeteria because they're not part of your group?

Don't allow group think to cause you to be hurtful or disrespectful. Be your own person and act according to your own moral code. Remember you are God's child—as are your coworkers—and you should treat your brothers and sisters in Christ the way your Father would want you to.

Group think also makes cliques incredibly unstable. This mind-set is easily swayed by leaders with charisma and charm, no matter how unscrupulous they may be. Since the group has no core values other than its own safety, it often responds in fickle or even cowardly ways. Perhaps the best example of this occurs with the Jewish populace of Jesus's day. They go from hailing Him as their King on Palm Sunday to demanding the release of Barrabas instead of Jesus a few days later. They shouted, "Crucify Him!" even though most of them knew He was an innocent man, not to mention the Son of God. They were influenced so much by yet another clique, the Jewish San-hedrin. This group perceived Jesus as a huge threat and were able to convince others that He should be killed.

If you pledge your allegiance to a clique or group in your workplace, you will eventually be turned upon just as Jesus was by the fickle crowd and fearful Jewish leaders. You will say something, do something, or simply no longer be needed. And suddenly you'll find that the group members to whom you've invested so much energy and so much time have turned their backs to you. You will then be the outsider that they laugh and gossip about. And while having the clique ostracize you is a blessing in disguise, it's still painful and potentially harmful to your primary purpose. If we are to become the men and women God created us to be, we must learn to think for ourselves, stand up for what is right, and pursue His agenda and not someone else's.

TIES THAT BIND

Another adverse effect of being connected to groups and cliques emerges as you get a reputation based on the group and not on who you really are. The group will quickly create a label for you. When you are affiliated with those who gossip, then it's logical that others will assume you're a gossip too. If you consistently hang out with the grumblers and complainers, most people will think you enjoy whining and want to avoid you.

Sometimes we don't even realize how enmeshed with our group at work we've become. We may not have realized the reputation that we've developed. In order to maintain an awareness of where you stand with groups at work, I encourage you to measure the connectedness to see if you are "tied" to these people. How much time do you spend discussing matters unrelated to work? How open is the group to other people joining in? What attracts you to the group? How does the group maintain your support and involvement? How much do members of the group influence your opinions of others in your workplace? How does the group enhance your work performance? Spend a few minutes thinking through your responses and jotting them down in a journal or notebook.

If you find yourself alarmed by your responses and your level of involvement with a certain clique or group at work, then I encourage you to gently sever the ties and reclaim your freedom and God's purpose for your presence in the workplace.

Cutting the cords of cliques won't be easy but will free you from the relationships and expectations that have encumbered you. You will be able to return your focus to performing the job for which you have been anointed and shake off the ties that bind.

FEED THE NEED ELSEWHERE

How do you detach yourself from the superglue that cliques seem to use in order to attract and attach their members? Becoming vigilant is one of the best ways. Simply remaining aware of the warning signs and ways cliques operate can allow you to sidestep them and avoid becoming ensnared. It's difficult to avoid getting bogged down in quicksand if you gradually walk into it unaware. Suddenly your steps begin sinking before you even realize what's happened, and then before long you're waist-deep in trouble. However, if you pay attention to where you step and stay on the path of righteousness, you will keep your momentum and reach your destination without delay. So separate yourself from situations and relationships that may have created labels for you and placed you under obligation. It may take awhile and a few polite "no thank you, not today" responses, but gradually you can be liberated.

Another way to avoid becoming ensnared in cliques is to make sure your relational needs are being met outside of the workplace. If you're starving for human connection and suddenly have opportunities to belong to a group of people who provide you with affirmation at work, you will be unlikely to resist. You must feed the need for friendship elsewhere. This is not to say that you shouldn't befriend coworkers or be pleasant and cordial with them. But you must not make this the place where you meet your primary needs for human relationship. You must remember that you are not at work to make friends and have a good time. If that happens as a by-product of performing your job, then that's a gift. However, we should not expect it or work to cultivate it.

God created families and friends for social support. I believe we are most susceptible to cliques and groups when our relational needs are not being met in appropriate ways elsewhere. Such a void in our lives can also set us up for office romances and illicit affairs. This is all the more reason to ensure that we have time away from the office to meet our personal needs for friendship, companionship, and intimacy.

We need to differentiate our relationships. Not all of them are on the same level and we must be aware that not all of them are afforded the same level of intimacy. Perhaps no one in Scripture models this better than Jesus. Consider the various individuals and groups that surrounded Him during His lifetime. First, Jesus has His beloved disciple John. They are best friends and can depend upon one another. Jesus is also very close with disciples James and Peter. These are the men who stood by Him during his agonizing ordeal in the Garden of Gethsemane.

They provided Him with a sense of family support and encouragement, especially during trials and tribulations.

We must make sure that we have people like this in our lives as well. Whether it's our immediate family, or a community of close friends who know us inside out, it's so important to have someone who is your confidante and soul friend, who loves you unconditionally and enjoys who you are. When you have the freedom to be yourself and know that you're appreciated and loved, you then become more empowered to take a stand against the cliques in your office. You won't need anything that they have to offer.

Next we see Jesus interacting with the rest of His twelve disciples. These men were crucial to His ministry and the fulfillment of His goals. This is where we see overlap between a personal and professional type of relationship. I believe this might be comparable to the individuals with whom you work most directly every day—your team, your department, your shift, your committee. You will have to interact on somewhat of a personal level with these folks just as part of professional courtesy. You learn their spouses' names, how many kids they may have, what hobbies they enjoy, and when their birthdays occur. You may like them and enjoy them or you may simply have to tolerate some of them. In this case I recommend using the personal connections to fuel the professional goals, not vice versa.

From the twelve disciples, we see Jesus commission the seventy in His name. "After these things the Lord appointed seventy others also, and sent them two by two before His face into every city and place where He Himself was about to go" (Luke 10:1). These people are commissioned and disseminated so that they can accomplish ministry goals, not to have a good time and form fast friendships with Jesus or with each other. They have a job to do. Jesus doesn't try to be close to them, to share in their lives on the same relational level as His disciples.

This is where we see a strong parallel to our situation in the workplace. Our coworkers are just that. We have common goals and are paid by the same employer; however, we don't need to have more in common than that. There are too many people in most offices to accomplish a level of personal friendship or intimacy with each other. Therefore, cliques spring up as a few begin to bond together and then another group forms in reaction to the first clique and so on and so on, each with its own agenda and preoccupation. It can be like high school all over again! The jocks and the brains, the popular kids and the geeks. Being a grown-up means moving beyond such labels and insecurity.

Returning to our Lord's example, next we see Him feed the five thousand and minister to countless others throughout His lifetime. He serves these people and doesn't expect to be fed by them. They don't have close proximity to Him or have access to His personal life. They experience His life-changing power through encounters that sometimes only last seconds. They didn't have to be with Him 24/7 to experience the profound effect of what He offered to them.

Similarly, there are hundreds if not thousands of people in your sphere of influence at work whom you may never even meet in person. Some corporations are so large that they can't have a company picnic because there's not a park big enough to hold them! Your customer base, the freelancers and subcontractors, the vendors and sales reps, on and on the chain goes. You're all united in common endeavors to fulfill the mission of your company, but you can't all be expected to connect personally.

With these levels in mind, I encourage you to feed your need for substantive, nourishing relationships off the job site. Like David found his Jonathan and Ruth had Naomi, you should have a special friend or community that supports you and thinks you're great. Then you will come to the office well fed emotionally and will be able to maintain a professional attitude that easily resists the pull of cliques. You will experience more peace because you're not scrambling to find something at work that it's not able to deliver. Maintaining a professional, respectful level of involvement with coworkers can spare you from the hazards of internal unrest.

HUMAN RESOURCES

The workplace can frequently be a toxic environment, and God has sent you there for training in His Kingdom, not to be swept into office politics or have personal needs met. While you must be able to interact with certain groups at work, you must also remain autonomous as you execute your Divine mission. God wants to elevate you and enlarge you, to expose you and mature you.

But maturity comes from accepting challenges responsibly and learning from mature people. If you have associations at your workplace with people who exhibit good work habits and have sharper skills than you, take note to see if it is someone whose position and professionalism allow you to glean from their expertise. Even as you seek to avoid cliques, you should be on the lookout for mentors and role models. These individuals usually enjoy teaching you what they've learned with no personal strings attached. They recognize your talent and potential and want you to grow and succeed.

While you remain vigilant for these kinds of people in your life, you should also watch for opportunities to learn new abilities. Sharpen your computer skills. Improve your ability to speak in front of groups. Take advantage of every training program and educational advantage your employer offers. Keep your focus on growth and development instead of developing relationships not intended for your improvement. Use your company's human resources to achieve Divine purposes!

Finally, you should realize that your next blessing is predicated upon tying into the next gift. On your job and in your life, watch for indications of other gifts. If you're so invested in your clique, you can easily miss the gift that God has placed in your path. David used everything he had; it doesn't appear that anything was lying dormant inside David! Rely on family and friends for your support and let the workplace remain your training ground. If you lock yourself into cliques and groups, opportunities may be right under your nose, but you'll miss them because you are distracted. Speak up and offer to take on a new responsibility if you feel you can handle it. Be willing to take a risk. Often gifts will surface as you are working on something entirely different. Speak with your employer and let him know that you would be willing to tackle something with a little different twist. Remember you are anointed and favor rests upon you!

The key to this commandment? Always maintain a pleasant, but professional, posture toward others in the work environment. Consider using the following prayer in your ability to resist the snares of cliques and groups in your workplace:

"Heavenly Father, I continue to be grateful for being in this position where You have placed me. Please empower me to fulfill Your mission and not to get caught up in my own agenda or the agenda of others. Allow me to resist the pull of cliques and groups that the enemy uses to distract and derail me. Remind me that my security is in You and You alone. Provide for my emotional and relational needs as I interact with my family, friends, and neighbors. Allow me to come to work emotionally full so that I can serve others instead of looking to meet my own needs. Help me to learn what You desire me to know in order to find my next gift. Strengthen those relationships where I can find a role model or mentor who will equip and strengthen me. I praise and thank You again for each and every one of the people with whom I work. Let me be a blessing to them this day. In Your Son's Precious Name, Amen."

TENTH COMMANDMENT:

ALWAYS KEEP YOUR
SONG NEAR YOU

HAVE you ever awakened first thing in the morning with some song stuck in your head? It may be the one blaring from your radio alarm clock, a melody you heard the day before, or a tune from years ago. Usually, it's some song that you would never have chosen yourself, a catchy pop number from the latest American Idol, a novelty song from some commercial or television show, or some rapper your kids forced you to listen to on their MP3 player. The melody becomes infectious and lingers with you throughout the day whether you want it to or not, filling your mind with its lyrics, your heart with its rhythmic beat, and your soul with its mood.

There's no denying that music can have an amazing power on how we feel and how we behave each day. It's no wonder that songs contribute so much to virtually every area of our lives: from a mother's tender lullaby to a Christmas carol, from a blues song in a nightclub to a sorrowful hymn at a funeral, from the upbeat soundtrack of our favorite movie to a love song we waltz to at our wedding. Everyone has their favorite kind of music and usually several favorite songs.

For me, there's nothing like the spontaneous riff of a jazz master or the harmonic blend of a gospel choir as it lifts the rich notes of some wonderful hymn off the page and into our ears. I love to stand in the pulpit at The Potter's House and hear the melodious strains of the spectrum of voices converging behind me as the soloist calls and the choir responds. God loves our songs of praise and delights as we turn our instruments and voices to Him as an expression of our joy, sorrow, gratitude, and ultimate triumph in His glory.

SOUL MUSIC

Just as we grow accustomed to the power of songs in various settings, we need to become aware of the song that God has placed inside us. You may not be musically inclined; others may turn their heads when they stand next to you in the choir. But each of us has a song that is all our own. Our job is to treasure this song, use it as a source of His joy, hope, and peace, and

THE TEN COMMANDMENTS OF WORKING

remember why He placed it within us. We should keep our song near us as a constant reminder that God's Spirit is alive and well in us. Jesus promised us that He would be with us until the end of time, and God sent His Spirit to dwell in us and transform us into His perfect creation. God has a plan for each one of us and the song He places in us is almost like a blueprint to keep us focused on His Divine design. He gives us soul music to sustain us. *He who began a good work in you will be faithful to complete it!* (Philippians 1:6).

It's undeniable that music is one of God's greatest gifts to us. And for those of us struggling in the hostile environment of our workplace, learning to keep the song that God has placed in our hearts alive can be the difference between our success and failure. There's nothing like having a song in your heart and a special "God-thing" in the pocket of your heart. Especially when the hostile darts of the enemy are zipping past us left and right. Satan is always out to steal our joy and to rob us of our peace. A song is a mighty powerful little weapon. It's an antidote for hateful people! A little *hmmmm* . . . is all it takes sometimes to just brush that speck of trouble right off the mat!

We have to keep these souls of ours anchored in the Lord. That inner sanctuary where only God can go has got to be guarded and filled with the Word so that the enemy stops dead in his tracks and reads the sign: NO ACCESS! Our song can serve as a heart security system, preventing the devil from breaking into an area where he has no business, or like the blare of a high-pitched siren, our song can be triggered by temptation and remind us of what our true heart's desire is.

The workplace is one place that the devil will somersault through, just jumping from one person to another, seeing who's most available. That's why being connected to God, not to people, is an absolute necessity! During those "hateful harangues," it might just be time to pause for a break and take your song with you outside or to the restroom, where a moment of Holy Ghost praying will clear the atmosphere and get the fog off your focus!

PREP TIME

Remember back in the old days when we used to frequent the clubs? Well, I do. I couldn't wait to get to the club. I started thinking about it around four o'clock in the afternoon, and when I did, I would just begin to hum and sing a bit. I was getting myself prepared for the atmosphere. Every last piece of clothing, down to the socks, was a decision; the whole thing had to be "cool." The preparation took some time, and every little detail was going to add to the "success" of the evening. By the time I got to the club, I was already in motion and was movin' to the beat! Some nights I'll bet that I spent as much time preparing for my night out at the club as the time I actually spent inside it on the dance floor!

I'm telling you about these days gone by because I want

to impart to you an important lesson. Just as I prepared my-self for a night at the club, so should Christians prepare themselves to step out into the world and into the work-place. Now, I don't mean you need to spend so much time getting dressed for work, but you do need to equip yourself to prepare for the battles you have to fight in your hostile work environment. This preparation should be time spent in God's presence. Study His Word, offer up some prayer, and of course, look deep inside yourself to call up your song and hum a few bars.

Are you spending the necessary time to prepare and equip yourself for what you face in the workplace? Do you know your song by heart so that it can naturally spring to your lips and feed your soul with its joyful melody?

Some of you may enjoy cooking and trying out new recipes from time to time. In many recipes I've noted that not only are the ingredients and directions included, but also the amount of time needed for preparation. We're used to paying attention to how long something has to simmer on the stove or bake in the oven, but unless we consider how long it takes to prepare, we may not allow ourselves enough time to complete the recipe. Similarly, when we are getting ready to walk into the fire of our hostile work environment, we must be adequately prepared and have put in the necessary time before God's presence. Our spiritual prep time must equal or exceed our time on the battlefield.

David knew this truth and was a well-equipped worshipper.

He had prepared himself in advance and came into the palace armed with his song. He was aware of the power that something so small and seemingly insignificant can have in accomplishing God's purposes. Also, you'll recall that when David killed the giant Philistine Goliath, he used only his slingshot and smooth stones as his weapons. In fact, he rejected Saul's armor and weapons and stayed with the weapons that were familiar and effective.

> So Saul clothed David with his armor, and he put a bronze helmet on his head; he also clothed him with a coat of mail.
>
> David fastened his sword to his armor and tried to walk, for he had not tested them. And David said to Saul, "I cannot walk with these, for I have not tested them." So David took them off.
>
> Then he took his staff in his hand; and he chose for himself five smooth stones from the brook, and put them in a shepherd's bag, in a pouch which he had, and his sling was in his hand. And he drew near to the Philistine.
>
> (I SAMUEL 17:38–40)

David didn't need to borrow someone else's weapons just because he was now faced with a heathen giant instead of a lion or bear threatening his sheep. Out of courtesy to the king, he tried on Saul's armor but knew that he had not tested it. He wasn't accustomed to its weight and the fit wasn't proper. David reminds us here that you don't need to prepare the way others think you should. You don't have to use their methods when your own have sufficed up until now.

His familiarity with his simple weapons helps to explain why David was victorious. He was well equipped. God will give His child enough spiritual ammunition and soul armor to take care of the trouble of the day.

VOICE YOUR VICTORY

Don't you wonder what David's song must have sounded like in the presence of a king afflicted by evil spirits? If you've ever heard someone play the harp, you know that it can indeed sound like the voice of angels.

While we might not know exactly what David's song before Saul sounded like, we can glimpse into the young shepherd king's heart by reading his poetry. From the collection of Psalms in the Bible, with the majority written by David, we gain insight into the kind of song that David kept in his heart. Whether in good times or in bad, in prosperity or poverty, in depression or in celebration, we see David turning to God and giving Him thanks and praise. David praises God for what He has done, what He is doing, and what He will do. There are enough verb tenses in the Psalms to keep my old high school English teacher in fits!

When David slays his enemies, he credits God's power for these victories. When David succumbs to his own lustful desires and commits adultery with Bathsheba and then has her husband killed, we see him confess his crimes before God, acknowledging that it's against his Lord that he has sinned. Whether grieving or rejoicing, David knows how to voice the victory he has in God's anointing. Ultimately, it is this confidence in God's goodness and sovereignty that nourish and sustain David throughout a lifetime of tragedy, trauma, and triumph. Through it all he remains able to sing the song that God first placed in his heart back on the hillsides outside of Bethlehem:

> Rejoice in the LORD, O you righteous!
> For praise from the upright is beautiful.
> Praise the LORD with the harp;
> Make melody to Him with an instrument of ten strings.
> Sing to Him a new song;
> Play skillfully with a shout of joy.
> For the word of the LORD is right,
> And all His work is done in truth.
> He loves righteousness and justice;
> The earth is full of the goodness of the LORD.
>
> (PSALM 33:1–5)

David expresses his exuberance over his realization of God's sovereignty and righteousness. It's as if those of us who know the Lord and are "upright" have no other fitting response to God's goodness than to praise and worship Him. With this kind of perspective, our joy cannot be dimmed by the darkness of the enemy. No matter how hostile our work environment becomes, we have the ultimate weapon within us.

If we can choose to praise God and trust that He is using us in our workplace despite how terrible it may seem to us, then we have a song that can shatter the spears and splinter the arrows that the enemy launches at us. Have you ever seen someone suffering terribly and yet in the midst of it they are still choosing to praise God? I recall a physically challenged gentleman and his wife who came to our church and asked for prayer. By the looks of this man, I assumed that he was most likely paralyzed or crippled as his wife pushed him in a wheelchair. "Perhaps he is here tonight to ask for healing," I thought to myself. Yet when I asked him what I could pray for him, he asked me to pray for his daughter who didn't know the Lord! It was plain to see two things as I looked this man of God in the eye. He knew what it meant to suffer both physically and mentally, and he knew our Father at an intimate level that I envied. He was a living testimony to God's glory by the way he handled the adversity in his life.

When others see us being joyful and resilient when there isn't good reason for it, when our circumstances are much the same as theirs in a difficult workplace, then they have to ask themselves, "What has she got to be happy about? What's the cause for that smile on his face and that twinkle in his eye?" God shines through us in such desperate places of darkness. The darker the night, the brighter His flame burns across the hillside. He wants us to take our light out from under the bushels of fear, shame, pride, or doubt and let it blaze before our coworkers.

PUMP UP THE VOLUME

Part of the reason many Christians struggle to keep their song near them in the workplace is that they've turned down the volume so low that they can barely hear God speak to them. When you spend more time in front of the television than in God's Word, it shouldn't surprise you that your song sounds faint as a whisper at times while the boom of popular culture in the media fills your thoughts. I don't want to make you feel guilty for not spending time in prayer and in feeding on the Word; the Holy Spirit is the only One who can convict you there. I simply want you to see the relationship between cultivating those elements of relationship with your Father and the sustaining of your song and strengthening of its melody. Turn up the volume of your prayers and the sound of your song will grow louder as well. Worship Him throughout your day and watch your joy and peace become a contagious remedy to the many germs of hostility floating through the office.

In addition, when we remain in open and direct communication with God, we will be able to hear His guidance, direction, and discernment for the many decisions that we're forced to make in our workplace. God will forewarn us and give insights and preparation that no counselor or friend has available. Our worship time will linger with us throughout our day and "ward off" evil spirits and attacks that come upon us by surprise. Our fears and doubts will melt as we immerse ourselves in the light of His truth. The Bible says that we are not to be "terrified by our adversaries" because *greater is He who is in us than he that is in the world* (I John 4:4).

Maybe you are on some mediocre job. Can you consider that God handpicked that job for you? Israel was confronted by the hostility of Egypt but God did not abandon His children. Instead He raised up Moses and Aaron to lead them out of Pharaoh's bondage and into the Promised Land. Esther, the queen, was placed in a hostile environment and forced to risk the wrath of her king in order to save her Jewish kinsmen. Over and over in Scripture, God makes it resoundingly clear. The greater the hostility, the greater the possibility! It's time to take a full inventory of all that God has placed within you and to discover the gross depth of the anointing that resides within you!

Grumbling, mumbling, and complaining will not usher us to the next level. This kind of expression attempts to negate our song by drowning it out in our heart with the sound of our own complaints. God has placed within us everything we need for the level we are at and the anointing to take us to the next. Instead of, "This job is not working. I cannot take another day of this! This isn't where I'm supposed to be. This can't be from

God!" sing God's praises for putting you in the place where you're most needed. Stop looking around at other people and take a look at yourself. Right where you are. God's enablement is within you; grace awaits you for your situation. You are a container for the very attributes of God Himself; the very giftings and talents of heaven He has divided up and distributed to His children as He chooses. You are no different. Pump up the volume and hear what He is doing in your life!

A NEW SONG

Wherever your lot has fallen, glorify God in it. That's the reason we are here. Stop complaining about your circumstances and look up at God and then within yourself! Our model of faith, the Lord Jesus, was placed in the most hostile of circumstances. The enemy was after Him before He was born, yet Jesus remarked, "I'm about my Father's business." The Bible says that if the princes of this world had known who He was, they would never have crucified the Christ! They had learned from His walk that the more they opposed Him, the more determined He became.

This is the kind of determination we must cultivate as we live out our faith. I remember years ago I was pastoring a group of people and some of them decided to curse the upcoming meeting we had planned. Well, I should have sent them a thank-you note afterward because it surpassed any previous meeting we had ever had at that church. God knows when the odds are against us, and what better time for Him to put His foot down and turn the situation around than when we are "in trouble." He promised that if we should call on Him "in trouble," He would deliver us. Anybody can praise God in happy times, but equate our relationship with the Lord to a marriage. Our marriage covenant includes the dry times, the sick times, and the poor times. How much more should our praise for God continue in all of those times, as well? We can spend too much time looking at everything and everyone but Him. Sing your song through the night and it will lead you to the Light!

I pray that this commandment has encouraged you to realize that God still has so much more planned for you. Begin to thank Him for all He has done and by faith for all He will do. Don't sell yourself short; there is still so much more in you regardless of how long your journey has been. Don't allow anything to separate you from the love of God—not discouragement, not illness or injury, not unemployment or bankruptcy, not divorce or devastation. If you've lost your song in the night, He'll give you a new song. Our boy David was well aware of this truth:

> I waited patiently for the LORD;
> And He inclined to me,
> And heard my cry.
> He also brought me up out of a horrible pit,

Out of the miry clay,
And set my feet upon a rock,
And established my steps.
He has put a new song in my mouth—
Praise to our God;
Many will see it and fear,
And will trust in the LORD.

(PSALM 40: 1–3)

Wait patiently, brothers and sisters, when you find yourself unable to remember the tune. He will always provide you with a new song, one that will sustain you on your journey even as it glorifies Him. God is for you! Stop the devil dead in his tracks by lifting your voice and praising the King who thought, and still does, that you are valuable enough to Him that He died to deliver you from hostility to holiness!

Consider singing this song of praise to Him and taking it with you into the hostile environment of your workplace:

"Lord, You have placed so much within me and continue to bestow so many blessings on my life. I thank You for the gift of Your song in my heart. I praise You for the joy it brings me and the way it reminds me of the Holy Spirit's presence in my heart. Allow me to keep my song near me at all times, but particularly as I enter the workplace and complete the job that You have anointed me to perform. If I've lost my song, help me to trust You to give me a new song. Use my song, Lord, to restore my joy and sustain my peace. Use my song so that others will see and hear and know that You are good and You are in control. Let the echoes of my song give You praise and glory long after I have left my present workplace and moved into the next level You are presently preparing for me. Thank You, Jesus, for all that You are! I pray this in Your holy name. Amen."

CONCLUSION:

EXIT INTERVIEW

THE nature of today's twenty-first-century working world is complex, multifaceted, and ever-changing. Some companies have evolved into a dressed-down, relaxed group of individuals who brainstorm in the office coffee shop and skateboard down the halls to one another's offices. Other corporations have become more conservative, maintaining a more formal dress code and upholding office decorum. The perspective with which individuals view their work has also evolved. Many people change jobs more often than they change hairstyles! Others continue to work in the same field, often for the same company, with a commitment similar to what their grandparents experienced. In the midst of all this variety, diversity, and individuality, work remains work—a position of fulfilling tasks and responsibilities in order to contribute to corporate goals and company mission statements. And a position of fulfilling tasks and responsibilities in order to be compensated for your contribution. Earning a decent wage is an honorable way to serve your family.

For us as believers, work also poses unique challenges and remarkable opportunities for us as we take Christ into the workplace with us. Often, but not always, we experience hostility and antagonism as our values, beliefs, lifestyles, and modes of operation clash with those of our coworkers and employers. In such environments, it's so tempting to become disheartened, discouraged, and disenfranchised.

Yet we are not to despair. Your presence in the workforce—your very position in the job that you hold today—is ordained by God as part of His plan for your life and the lives of those around you. As we have seen throughout all ten of these commandments, you are gifted with special and unique abilities that He delights in using in your workplace. He anoints you for your work and empowers you to carry His methods into a world darkened and dismayed by the presence of the enemy of our souls. You are indeed the man for the job! You are the one and only woman for the job!

In many companies, when you leave your job to take another, the human resources department will conduct an exit interview with you. This is an opportunity for each of you to learn from the experience of your time with this employer. You are given the opportunity to voice your suggestions for increased efficiency and improved performance in the company. Your supervisor is given the chance to review your strengths and weaknesses and, hopefully, to commend you on a job well done and wish you success in your new venture. Overall, it can be a very positive, inspiring time of communication and exchange of ideas.

While you and I can't have the same kind of dialogue—there's so much more that I wish I could share with you in person—I have tried to be concise in distilling God's message into each commandment. Please indulge me in a quick review of all ten areas of truth that we have covered in these pages:

1. Know That You Are Anointed for the Job or Position You Now Hold!
2. Don't Expect to Be Appreciated
3. Embrace Opportunities for Change
4. Do the Job Well While Remembering the Vision
5. Don't Let the Environment Get Inside of You!
6. Increase Your Capacity to Work with Difficult Personalities
7. Where You Are Is Not Where You Are Going!
8. Achieve Optimal Results with Minimal Confusion
9. Do Not Pledge Allegiance to Cliques and Groups!
10. Always Keep Your Song Near You

I encourage you to make note of which of these commandments address your current issues and speak directly to your heart. You may want to spend some time discussing, journaling, and praying through what you've learned and been reminded of in these chapters. Please keep these handy and turn to them often as a way of remembering eternal Truth and not momentary affliction. Take these commandments with you and use them as a lifeline for discovering your destiny and fulfilling His purposes.

My wish is that you feel enlightened, inspired, and energized as you go back into your workplace. I hope you feel better equipped to handle the hostilities that have discouraged and disarmed you in the past. My prayer is that God will use these ten commandments to produce ten times the blessings you will receive in your workplace by honoring Him and living out your anointing.

As we conclude our exploration of these commandments that God has placed upon my heart to share with you, I pray that He would speak to you and use these words to strengthen your resolve and inspire your performance in the position that He has placed you in. May you be nourished and refreshed by the example of David and by the other biblical truths that reinforce these commandments. May your workplace be just a little brighter because you carry the truth of these commandments—His words, not mine—inside you. May your song sound a little stronger in the midst of the chaotic din of the workplace. May you confront the hostility, not with fear or trepidation, but with the hope, joy, and peace that Christ has placed in you to illuminate Himself to the world.

Workplaces may always pose hostile environments for us as Christians. However, we need not be afraid or anxious about our role in the job to which we're called. God instills us with His power, not with fear over what has happened, what could happen, or what might happen. Worry and doubt are tools of the enemy in his attempts to undermine our ability to carry out the mission that God has given us. If you take these ten commandments to heart and practice them as best you can, I won't promise that you will struggle less in your workplace. In fact, you may even struggle more and experience even greater hostility because you'll recall that the greater the hostility, the greater that possibility! God takes great pleasure in redeeming circumstances that others intended for evil. The enemy doesn't like it when we become more equipped with the armor of God. He will get out his bigger weapons and try to frighten and intimidate us with new trials and unpleasant surprises.

If you practice these ten commandments, however, I can assure you that you will experience new levels of peace, joy, and hope as you bask in God's presence and exult in His Divine design for all that you do. You will experience more confidence and more excitement over the incredible journey upon which you've embarked. You will wake up each morning knowing your life is purposeful and your job has meaning. He has a plan for you, for your good and not for evil, and you are in the midst of fulfilling it right this very moment as you read this page.

Dear brothers and sisters, I charge you to go forth into your workplace, no matter how hostile it may be, bathed in His anointing, knowing that you are blessed and highly favored! I wish you Godspeed on your journey and joy along the way!